To Shalin!
I see you miss —
Dnt be afraid to be
Star that you are!
xoxo,
Taiia

Famous!

How to Be the Star of Your Show

A Teen Girl's Guide to Embracing Her Fabulous Self

TAIIA SMART YOUNG

Taiia Smart Young/Smart Girl Media
www.TaiiaSmartYoung.com

Cover Design: Ana Grigoriu
www.books-design.com

Photographer: Jerome Shaw
www.photosbyrome.com

Layout: Quill Pen Editorial Services
www.quillpeneditorial.com

Ordering information for quantity sales:
Special discounts are available on quantity purchases by schools, youth organizations, non-profits and others. For specifics, contact Smart Girl Media via the Contact Us page at the website above and write "quantity sales" in the subject line.

Famous! How to Be the Star of Your Show: A Teen Girl's Guide to Embracing Her Fabulous Self by Taiia Smart Young –1st edition

ISBN: 978-0-9962830-0-7 (paperback)
ISBN: 978-0-9962830-1-4 (ebook)

XO

To my baby sister, Anika. You know how we use movies and TV shows to create our own language? Cristina Yang said this about Meredith Grey on *Grey's Anatomy*:

"She's my person. If I murdered someone, she's the person I'd call to help me drag the corpse across the living room floor. She's my person."

Nik, you are my person. Then. Now. Always.

(P.S. I'm soooo not the murdering type, so you're completely safe. Plus, we're not built for jail.)

SHOUT OUTS

It's not the Grammys or the Oscars, so there's no need to thank the Academy, but I'm grateful to the Most High for this gift. The following people deserve all kinds of accolades, gold trophies, and interpretive dances (you know I'll do it!) because they've taught me that love is a verb. So when I get it, I give it.

To Shateek Young, my ride-or-die hubby, thank you for laughing at my shenanigans, reeling me in from the edge, helping me think clearly, and sustaining me with unshakable faith. You're the best for letting me pound away—undisturbed—on my computer, and ramble on like a madwoman when I needed to vent. Even when I did my best to pretend that everything was okay, you saw past my amateur acting skills and hugged me. They just don't make 'em like you anymore. This love is unbreakable, word to Alicia Keys.

I get all mushy thinking that Lil Sha, a.k.a. the No. 1 Son, a.k.a. The Birthday Thief chose me to be his mother and teach valuable lessons about motherhood. You see life through a very special lens and I'm (slowly!) learning to appreciate it. One thing is for sure: You're a work of art, a masterpiece.

My mother, Enid K. Crowder, was my first editor and the first person to take me seriously when I announced my plan to become a writer. You bought me the tools: books, computers, printers, ink cartridges, and endless reams of paper. But most of all, you believed it was possible, encouraged me to send my stories into the world and work toward my goal. As a know-it-all teen, I didn't understand your sacrifices, but now I do. Because of you, I can.

Anika Locklear, my baby sister, is my ace. You're so crown for understanding when I go from super serious to macadamia nuts in the same conversation. Forget pig Latin, you speak Tee. I hope Jean "Jay-R" Cidone understands the late night and early morning phone calls and text messages. That's just how we do.

I call my late grandmother's name, Sojourner Taiia Knight, because I believe that when we call the names of our ancestors they rise to be present with us. That said, you're probably tired of hearing from me, Grandma. I miss talking to you about everything from current events to the Wu-Tang Clan. Like Andraé Crouch sang, "I'll be thinking of you."

My dad, Ronald Locklear Sr., is my first example of a bona fide money-making entrepreneur who wasn't too cool to cook, clean, drop us off at school, and provide structure. I still watch *Mr. Mom* and think about how you did all the stuff Michael Keaton did in the film with ease—and made it fun, even when the "warden" said no. Priceless.

My brother, Ronald Locklear Jr., is a fellow creative and constant supporter. Thanks for sending long-distance love. It never goes unnoticed and it's always appreciated. You're the highest of the high. Don't ever wonder.

Mi familia, mi corazón: I'm beyond blessed with a cast of wonderful characters who support me and keep me highly entertained. I'm so glad the cameras aren't rolling when we're together!

To my *Juicy* magazine family: Me and you us never part makidada. You ladies are the ultimate get-it-done crew. I love our relationship conversations, reality TV recaps and middle of the day screenings. The support and encouragement throughout this process has been amazing. #squad

Ah, but what about my friends? I won't be careless and forget anyone's name here. Nope, you won't call me up later to give me the business for that. No ma'am. No sir. Just know this, y'all inspire me with your individuality, intelligence, resilience, and dedication.

Allow me to brag about my dynamic sorors of Delta Sigma Theta Sorority, Inc. and the dedicated members of the Brooklyn Alumnae Chapter. You divas sent flowers and encouraging emails, invited me to speak at your schools and churches, and allowed me to participate in the book fair when *Famous!* was just a Word document on my computer. I'm humbled by your generosity. You truly embody scholarship, sisterhood, and service.

Clarence Haynes and Nira Hyman, my editor and copy editor, respectively, put professional polish on my words, so that nothing was lost in translation. Without you two, I'd look real basic right now, instead of all kinds of fabulous.

And to you, Star: Thanks for hanging out with me. I cherish your company. There's more to come and in the words of Bruno Mars, "Don't believe me? Just watch."

ALLOW ME TO
REINTRODUCE MYSELF
(INTRO)

Confession: I'm not famous, but you've probably realized that from the cover of this book. Um, scratch that, I'm not well known in a way that would make reporters break their necks to stick a mic in my face if I strutted across the red carpet at MTV's Video Music Awards. They'd probably ignore me or think I was a handler who'd carelessly lost her A-list client, but they would be so wrong.

Although I'm not a celebrity in the traditional sense, I am the star of my show.

I'm a writer/editor who's worked for ESSENCE, XXL, and Juicy magazines, and a cool nonprofit devoted to empowering girls. But we'll get to that in a minute. I co-launched Juicy, the first celeb life, hair, and beauty magazine for women of color with one of my besties, Paula T. Renfroe. I've spent loads of time researching, writing, interviewing, and studying celebrity shenanigans—and testing my fair share of conditioner, mascara, and lip gloss too—and hiring interns, as I've done with several previous jobs.

Some of these interns looked amazing on paper, but once they got the internship, their true colors came out and it wasn't all rainbows and gold-colored glitter. More like something from Darth Vader's dark side. Luckily, there were girls and guys who were super-confident, smart, and always hungry to learn more. Those interns were always my faves and some of them became my mentees. Something about my vibe has encouraged bosses, teachers, co-workers, organizers, and leaders to invite me to speak at their schools and graduations, and give interactive workshops to their teen groups. I'm a big sister in real life, so offering advice goes with the territory. And let's face it, we're all better off when someone says: "Uh, don't go down that street, Dorothy. It's a dead end, but this yellow brick road right here will be just fine for those fancy ruby slippers you are wearing."

Even when I took a short break from magazine publishing, my heart gravitated toward young people. As the director of content for shine365.com, I covered anti-violence, tolerance, and bullying prevention topics, and we had blogs before everybody and their grandma decided to create one. Later, as the Assistant Director of Communications and Marketing at Girls Inc. (the organization that inspires all girls to be strong, smart, and bold), I selected participants for the Girls Advisory Board (GAB). I travelled with GAB annually to Washington, D.C., to talk to their Congressional leaders about teen pregnancy, lack of afterschool programs, and other hot topics. So if you're asking, what does all of this mean, T? It means empowering young women (and young men) is my passion. It energizes me. It means I've been your A-1 since Day-1 and you didn't even know it. Now you do.

Let me clarify what being the star of my show means. I've spent a lot of time figuring out how to be comfy cozy in my skin and getting to know who T is without worrying what other people think about me. It's too much pressure to meet everybody's expectations, especially if you don't know what you expect from yourself, right? And as my girl Shailene Woodley brilliantly told *Vanity Fair* magazine, "It's not my business what other people think of me." All right now, Shailene, I totally agree.

But I didn't do this self-reflection thing in an annoying, navel-gazing way. It was definitely trial and error, but I made conscious choices about who I wanted to be and the experiences I wanted to have vs. just going with the flow of whatever my friends were doing. And I was fortunate that my mother supported me, even if she didn't always agree! I've learned so much along the way and developed five core beliefs, including:

1. Confidence is my best accessory.
2. Advice from my crew, a.k.a. my Fave Five, is essential (this is a group of seasoned vets who are much wiser than I am).
3. Choose my own adventure, even when others doubt what I'm doing.
4. Failure, no matter how much it hurts and feels like death, is a part of success.
5. Define myself for myself. I'm the author of this dictionary.

Little did I know that these rules would become the foundation for being the star of my show and inspire me to write a book. When I interview folks like Jordin Sparks, Zendaya, Wendy Williams, Chris Rock, Jada Pinkett Smith, and Kerry Washington, I've found that they share similar principles. Talking to them is always interesting, especially when we discuss their backstory. You know, life before the exclusive parties, overly hyped award shows, and trips to the Cannes Film Festival became part of their routine. Before the spotlight was cast on them, they were "nobody," grinding their way to be somebody that everybody talked about. Actually, they were already stars, building confidence, consulting with trusted experts, falling flat on their face, and deciding which projects to reject, accept, and explore. They were tapping into their star power. That jolt of internal electricity guides their footsteps.

You have it too. And I'd rather you #bethestarofyourshow than be a supporting actress, or worse, an extra in someone else's blockbuster production.

The idea for *Famous!* was cooked up from three places: my personal escapades, girls who've asked me for advice, and conversations I've had with celebrities. My goal is to inspire you to discover, declare, and active your star power. So lemme give you the scoop before you dive into these pages. This book is a gumbo of personal stories from me, tips, and activities with plenty of space for you to scribble your thoughts. If you need more room, whip out your journal and have at it. I've also included stories from my Star Crushes, like Mo'ne Davis, an extraordinary Little League pitcher with a mean ol' arm. Mo's gifted, but she's also focused and determined.

Each chapter kicks off with a quote. I'm all about messages that get right to the point, but stay with me forever, and yes, I'm one of those sappy chicks who think certain song lyrics were written especially for me. I'm positive that when Janelle Monáe sings: "Even if it makes others uncomfortable, I will love who I am," she penned that line in "Queen" for me and only me. Anyway, I post a ton of quotes on Instagram, and I've included some of my faves from Mama Oprah and funny lady Amy Poehler here. Then, each chapter ends with a *Famous!* Cheat Sheet, a specific place to include your feelings about confidence, ignoring labels, failure, and success.

I'm a pop culture junkie (really I'm an info junkie, but whatevs) who's fascinated by everything from Beyoncé's work ethic (bow down) to how Nasty Gal founder Sophia Amoruso became a fashion and ecommerce powerhouse to Netflix's business model, so expect stories from change makers we can't stop talking about. Learning how companies and celebrities zoom past the competition, chart their own course, and make moolah is excellent motivation for your star story.

You've probably guessed it by now, but I've remixed the concept of fame. *Famous!* isn't about everybody knowing you, it's about you knowing yourself. That type of recognition lasts beyond the fifteen minutes folks are so desperate to have—it lasts a lifetime. Are you ready, Star? Let's go.

THROWBACK THURSDAY

"If you don't define yourself for yourself, you'll be crushed into others' fantasies and eaten alive."

—AUDRE LORDE

My shiny new beginning starts at the end of an important moment in my life. This is a coming-of-age movie flashback, so stay with me. Picture yours truly cast as the protagonist, a quiet sixth grader, pitted against my antagonist: Mr. Nas, a.k.a. the evil villain. Truthfully speaking, he wasn't wicked at all, but you couldn't tell me that at the time because I was all in my feelings.

Anyway, my grades were super good and I was on track to be the valedictorian of my elementary school. The word sounded huge, regal, intimidating, and too big to fit in my little mouth, and the idea of speaking at graduation scared me a little bit, but I *knew* I could do it. Teachers loved me. If you looked up *studious* in the dictionary, you'd see a picture of me with poofy bangs, a messy ponytail, and a huge Kool-Aid grin. No one complained about me being too loud or too annoying. Sadly, my teachers, including Mr. Nas, informed my mother that I was so quiet they'd sometimes forget that I was even in the room.

Yes, as in i-n-v-i-s-i-b-l-e.

Way to make an impression, right?

So Mr. Nas gifted my valedictory speech to My Friend, who probably had no idea that the job originally belonged to me. Announced it like it was no big deal. Handed it over, like, *Thanks for studying your butt off and being an upstanding student, but we've selected the girl with full control of her outdoor voice.* I don't remember his exact words, but I remember how I felt. My face caught fire. My chest stung. My throat choked on words. My eyes spurted tears. A little piece of me died that day.

Crushed didn't begin to describe the tornado of hurt, anger, and jealousy swirling around my skinny little body. All those years of being quiet, shy, and playing by the good-girl rules (oh, and let's not forget being invisible) had finally collided and knocked me off my feet. What hurt most was that I adored Mr. Nas and thought we belonged to this student-teacher mutual admiration club, especially as he'd selected me multiple times as Student of the Week, praised how many books I could devour in a month, and complimented my vocabulary skills. I knew what it felt like to be passed over to play volleyball in gym—but I didn't care because I was never a huge fan of the sport and could deal with that—but this was something different. It was an opportunity for my teacher to guide me as I pushed myself into new territory, but this told me that he didn't think I had it enough guts to survive this challenge. He'd considered me too fragile to speak at the podium in front of an auditorium brimming with family, faculty, and friends. And at the time, I was too scared to disagree, speak up for myself, or simply fight back.

But as that old saying goes: When one door closes, somewhere a window opens. It sounds corny, but it's absolutely true.

As fate would have it, that same week I won the How a Book Makes Me Feel Contest, and the vice principal asked me to recite my winning entry at graduation. Call this the all-important second chance to make a *real* first impression. My mother, a social butterfly and covert perfectionist, insisted that I master the speech until it leaked out of my ears. With me rewriting the script and Ma as the director, the plot on this movie was about to change, big time.

I got to work on my speech, underlining words that required special emphasis, like jokes and key phrases, and I practiced looking at my imaginary audience. "Make eye contact! Speak up!" Ma instructed. "I need the parents in the back row to hear you. Good. Now do it again."

And I did.

What else could I do at crunch time? Two things: Go big or go home, dragging my shy tail between my legs. My first few attempts were craptacular. I sucked, but Ma coaxed me into doing it again and again... and I got better. I got louder. I got stronger. Truthfully, I got sick of hearing myself. BUT I DID NOT STOP. I said that speech so many times that I didn't need the paper in front of me: The words were etched on my brain.

On graduation day, I trotted to the podium in a white lace dress with baby's breath flowers tucked into my tight curls to recite my How a Book

Makes Me Feel essay. Palms dripped sweat. Heart pounded like a marching band coming down 34th Street during the Macy's Thanksgiving Day Parade. As my shoes clicked toward the stage, I prayed for the school to fall into a sinkhole or a million deadly bees to sting everyone, including me. Not kidding. The only thing that calmed my nerves was this thought: I had prepared for this. This was the first step to becoming the star of my show.

So I took a deep breath, wiped my sweaty hands on my pretty dress, glanced at the crowd, thought about Mr. Nas and My Friend with her booming voice, and I freakin' *slayed* like a vampire having her first neck-bone sandwich. I had to. I had to show Mr. Nas that I could do this, but most of all, I had to prove it to myself. The audience listened, laughed at my jokes, and clapped. Maybe you didn't hear me. They clapped—for *me*, the Shy Girl with invisible tendencies—during my first time at the podium.

But wait. There's more.

After graduation, my family stood in the school's concrete courtyard, and as Ma fixed my corsage, Mr. Nas walked over and apologized to me in front of my family. He said: "I didn't know you had it in you."

The Shy Girl inside of me wanted to scream at the top of her lungs:

HOW COULD YOU KNOW?

YOU NEVER ASKED!

YOU DIDN'T EVEN OFFER TO HELP ME FIND MY VOICE!

But Ma would've flipped out if I spoke to an adult like that. So I smiled, one of those tight-lipped, toothless grins, and said, "Thank you." And that was the last time I allowed someone to underestimate me, or crush me into his (or her) tiny box of who and what I should be. I narrowly escaped being "eaten alive," as the poet Audre Lorde so eloquently put it. That whole situation could've destroyed me, but it didn't. Deep down I always knew I was so much more than just the Shy Girl. I never labeled myself this way, but others did and it just kinda stuck.

I'd be lying if I said everything was all good after the credits rolled on my little sixth-grade movie. It wasn't. I was twelve. Life got complicated. There were more hurdles to jump over and sometimes I fell hard. But every day after that graduation day, I made an effort to be the star of my show, until it became second nature, like it is now.

These days friends and family tell me that I laugh too loud at comedies, or that I hog the living room floor when we're playing *Just Dance*. Do I make too much noise? Yep. Do I dominate the floor? Yep. And that's okay, because that's all part of my *star* power. Don't worry about me: I got this.

BREAKDOWN

1

CONFIDENCE IS THE NEW BLACK, BOO

"Know yourself and you will win all battles."

—SUN TZU

I'm an accessories girl. Bracelets. Rings and thangs. Big chains. Two chains. A big ol' faux gold ring in the shape of a half-moon makes me feel good. No judgments, please! But my absolute ultimate accessory wasn't purchased in a store. It's something I was born with and I've been tweaking it forever, ever. It's a simple but complex word: It's called confidence. Now when you love accessories and are daring enough to try new trends and the color of the year (raise your hand if this is you), it's easy to believe retail therapy can be the answer to a self-esteem boost. It isn't. It's just a fun, temporary fix.

The rush from scooping up a double arm cuff from Forever 21 fades. Fast. Never mind what the fashion forecasters said about rocking that army candy, hemline, or a must-wear hue, because confidence is the new black and it, unlike beautiful shades that come and go, like 2015's Marsala, confidence will never go out of style. Your insides, that combo of brains, intuition, talent, moxie, and adventurousness are the ingredients that make you one-of-a-kind special. It'll never get old or be deemed so last season. It's what fashionistas call a classic.

Confidence. What is it really, anyway? I mean, we think we know, right? It's a ten-letter word that simply means: You believe in yourself. But there's so much more to it. When you believe in yourself, you're willing to step outside the safety of that warm, cozy comfort zone to try new foods (cronuts!), have unique experiences (rock climbing), and take risks (audition for the talent show!). No one wakes up with her confidence meter on a hundred thousand trillion—unless she's related to Kanye West or something–but I'm sure even Yeezy has his off days too (privately, of course). His level of confidence, or should I say, Kanye-fidence, doesn't even measure on a regular scale. (Side note: If you listen closely to 'Ye's lyrics, especially from *The College Dropout*, he reveals some of his insecurities, but that doesn't stop him from saying and believing he's the best. Let's not forget this is the "creative genius" with legendary rants and bizarre quotes, such as: "I'm like a vessel, and God has chosen me to be the voice and the connector," or "I am Shakespeare in the flesh.")

Confidence isn't feel-good magic; once you have it, you're not necessarily stuck in a particular zone—operating at a six out of ten, for instance—for life. No, confidence levels need to be constantly tested and explored. You control how high the number soars and how low it dips.

Conceit, Perfection & Fear Can Go That Way →

Having a healthy dose of self-confidence doesn't mean you're conceited, perfect, or fearless. First, conceit is confidence's no-good cousin who only comes around to be all braggy and self-centered. This girl is annoying. When she comes to town you're always busy doing important stuff, like counting the number of hairs in your eyebrows. That's how badly you don't want to see this one.

Second, let's deal with the concept of perfection. Perfection is a myth. It's limiting and claustrophobic. It doesn't leave room for screwing up and learning from mistakes. Plus, it's exhausting to try living up to the pressure of saying and doing the right thing all the freakin' time. You're a teen. Mistakes are part of the program.

Third, there's this notion that confident girls are fearless. Honestly, I like this one in theory, but in reality we're all fearful of something—spiders, public speaking, flying, or going to the dentist. You either let fear prevent you from doing something dope, like flying to Spain with the school choir, or basic, like seeing the dentist before the cavity creeps have a field day on your enamel. Hmm. Decisions, decisions.

I prefer to think of fear as **F**alse **E**vidence **A**ppearing **R**eal. I don't know who originally said this—believe me I researched it, because every life coach, celeb, and motivational speaker uses it—but it's true. It's an obstacle blocking you from putting on that umpire's mask, testing your jokes at the teen comedy club or showing someone other than your bestie the robot you built from scratch. Fear can seep into your head and keep you from being the brilliant Star that you are. Even the confident girl at school who swears she can sell ice to Eskimos gets scared. Your heroes, your favorite celebrities aren't fearless. But they take action anyway. They push past their fear because the reward is better than whatever scares the crap out of them, i.e. a dentist carrying snakes on a plane.

But enough about my ideas of conceit, perfection, and fear, because I know you get it. To be confident, you don't need a thousand tips; more like a few tried-and-true ones to help you crush it on a regular basis.

★★★ Star Tips ★★★

1. **Change something:** The easiest way to feel powerful and confident is to successfully affect change. It doesn't have to be a huge change, at first. A small one will do. Think about it. Are you always running late? If so, why? What do you need to do to avoid racing around the house looking for your sneakers and sweats on gym day? How can you prepare more easily? It may be as simple as checking the weather and ironing clothes the night before (or even the week before) and putting your sneakers in your backpack. If you wear a uniform to school, this task is even easier because you aren't challenged to find a specific outfit for every day of the week. Don't underestimate the power of planning ahead. If three inches of snow will cover your city on Wednesday, start attacking the junky hallway closet for those boots

days before the storm.

2. **Be prepared:** You can't expect to have this newfound confidence without preparation. It just doesn't work that way. So if the goal is to make the swim team this year, then you need to ask yourself a bunch of questions, including: How many hours per day do I need to practice? When will I practice? What are my strengths? Who can help me improve in my challenge areas? Or maybe the goal is to take home first prize in the science fair. Think about this: Which experiments earned top honors for the last three years? How can my experiment best show off my skills? What should I include to impress the judges? Look, even if it's as simple as making a birthday dinner for your brother after he's announced he's vegan, preparation is huge. You need groceries and that doesn't include four pounds of chopped meat; grab the tofu and veggies instead.

3. **Ask for it:** Start small, then graduate to something more difficult. This helps us build faith in ourselves. Tomorrow, ask your teacher for a chance to redo that crappy *Of Mice and Men* paper. Maybe you'll ask for that cutie's phone number or you'll organize the next school fund-raiser. This is particularly a big deal if you don't usually assert yourself. Don't wait for someone to recognize that you're the best person to arrange the fund-raiser, because you'll be waiting forever. The worse you can possibly hear is no. We've all heard no before. Yes, it stings and can be embarrassing, but it's part of life. No one escapes school without being rejected at least one hundred times. Wait. I made that up. But if it were true, you'd feel better because you've heard no 30 times already.

4. **Define yourself:** This is way more complex than knowing you prefer ice cream to sorbet. (We'll dig into this later.) That's a cute factoid, but it doesn't speak to who you are at the core. It means being able to honestly answer the "Who am I?" question without filtering the response for your friends or parents, or shrinking when bullies attack your weight, clothes, or the sound of your voice. Bullies dislike confidence. It's their kryptonite. Don't get caught up in other folks' chatter and definitions, either. We're quick to slap a label, like band chick, on someone or put her in a box, like shy girl, simply because it's easy, because it's all we see. Playing the saxophone is probably a small

part of who that person really is. The person who knows you best is you. Here's the good news: The defining process is an ongoing situation. You'll learn more about yourself every time you succeed and fail. There's an activity later in this chapter to encourage you to begin the process of defining yourself—in your own words.

5. **Get used to hearing "no":** Watching an entitled girl have a meltdown when someone tells her "no" is so irritating. It makes me wonder: *Didn't your mother ever tell you "no" when you were a kid?* Yes, rejection hurts. It's discouraging and infuriating, but it's part of what my favorite lion Mufasa described as the "circle of life." My suggestion is to build a thick skin, don't take anything personally, use rejection to step up your game, and keep on pushing. Don't let it break you. No is just a word. Twelve publishers rejected J.K. Rowling and her story about a boy wizard named Harry Potter. The first book—at three hundred and twenty pages—was considered too long for a children's title and it was headed for the rejection pile when an assistant spotted Rowling's illustrations and convinced an agent to sign her. This is proof that success is possible, even when people don't immediately see your vision. When a "no" flips into a "yes," the outcome can be amazing. Keep going.

6. **Act like you want it:** Your mindset has to line up with everything else that you're doing. It's difficult to move forward if you doubt your ability to deliver an oral presentation in class. Kick the negative thoughts out of your head. Replace them with positive mantras: "I can do this." "I'm prepared." "I'm ready to own this moment." How you feel about speaking in front of your classmates will reveal itself in your voice, volume, and posture. Why should they pay attention if you're mumbling into the paper with slumped shoulders? You should expect them to zone out! The best way to get their attention is to speak with authority, make eye contact, and talk loud enough so that the kid in the back of the classroom secretly downloading a new app can hear you. When you change your actions (i.e. show that you're self-assured), people change how they respond to you.

7. **Believe in yourself:** What good is defining yourself, being prepared, and kicking doubt in the butt if *you* don't believe in yourself? Allow me to answer

that for you: It isn't any good. I'm not saying that you won't have doubts, but you have to build your belief system every day so that it overpowers those negative thoughts. You can do this by focusing on where you already excel, or discovering where you'd like to excel. I'm truly impressed by (and jealous of!) the kids on *MasterChef Junior*. The youngest ones are eight years old and they cook restaurant-quality meals. I know it took plenty of burnt or undercooked recipes before any of them became good at making Chilean sea bass with wilted spinach and baby eggplant. None of those kids walked into a kitchen with amazing knife skills. They had to practice and believe they could do it—and so did their families and friends.

One of my absolute favorite stories of confidence meets natural talent, meets opportunity, meets willpower comes from ballerina Misty Copeland. Misty is the American Ballet Theatre's first black soloist in two decades. She wasn't always the confident ballerina known for leaping across the stage in *The Nutcracker* and *Sleeping Beauty*. She was a shy (her words, not mine), 13-year-old girl who learned ballet at a Boys & Girls Club in California. What could've been just a class and a chance for her to escape her chaotic home life (she was sleeping on a motel room floor with her five siblings) became a life-changing moment. Her ballet instructor Cynthia Bradley recognized that Misty was gifted. In an interview with *ABC News*, Misty said, "It was probably the worst time in my childhood when ballet found me." She added, "Having someone believe in me is why I think I dove into it." Sometimes, another person can see you in a way you cannot see yourself. Because Cynthia was confident in Misty's ability, it pushed the ballerina to work hard to meet her teacher's high expectations.

While it takes most dancers several years to make sure their ankles, feet, and legs are strong enough to dance on their toes en pointe, Misty danced en pointe within three months of taking her first class. Most girls start at age five and study at schools that prepare them for entry into places like London's The Royal Ballet or the Paris Opera. But after little more than a year or so of training, Misty was good enough to perform professionally. I knew bits of Misty's story, but it didn't truly sink in how hard she fought to rise to the top of her game as a classically trained ballerina until I saw her in Under Armour's "I Will What I Want" advertising campaign.

If you haven't seen it, it's required viewing on YouTube and it's way more inspiring than some dog doing the cha-cha. The commercial starts with a voiceover of a little girl reading a rejection letter, while the camera is focused on Misty's incredibly strong, muscular legs. The letter is a combination of all the reasons people said she couldn't be a dancer: You have the wrong body type. Your feet are too big. You're too muscular. By the end of the commercial, Misty goes from being in a dance studio to a stage with bright lights. She's flying, graceful legs and arms slicing through the air.

It takes a lot for me to cry during a movie, but this commercial left me reaching for tissues. Misty's story is so important because of her confidence and her *willpower*. She was active, not passive. Misty did more than just wish for a chance to be a ballerina. She worked for it. It took practice, commitment, and dedication. It required her to replace fear with focus. Misty had to define herself in ways that people with limited vision couldn't see. She could've let someone's comment about her feet being too big interrupt her destiny, or mess with her self-confidence. Instead she's making history and changing the way people perceive ballerinas.

Believe In Your Flyness...Conquer Your Shyness

It's everything to have the support of your family and friends, but don't forget to celebrate yourself too. In Kanye-speak, that means believe in your flyness. I ride hard with him on this one. One way to express this is with a best-self collage, a specific type of vision board dedicated to celebrating all the things you do well. Every girl needs a best-self collage when fear and doubt attempt to threaten her progress. Before starting your collage, fill in the blanks below. Feel free to create your own fill-in-the-blank sentences too. Type them up and print it or scribble them in a notebook. Just know you'll need to add them to your collage.

I feel amazing when I:

_____

_____

_____

I love myself because I'm:

_____

_____

_____

I am:

_____

_____

_____

Supplies

- An open mind (gushing with ideas)
- Curiosity
- Theme music (any playlist that makes you feel empowered)
- Cardboard or oaktag
- Glue or tape
- Scissors
- Fill-in-the-blank answers
- Fave, inspirational quotes (these can be from a story, poem, song or rap lyric)
- Magazines (grab a bunch of different ones—fashion, travel, music, beauty)
- Three different photos (make copies!) of when you felt confident/proud
- Cell phone

Step 1: Crank up that playlist. Get into the zone.

Step 2: Flip through the mags and tear out pictures that connect with your vision. Example: If you dream about being an author, find the book review section in one of those magazines and tear that out. Add images of authors too. Feel free to include items that make you feel good about yourself, plus goals you plan to accomplish, like learning how to swim. Rip out the page with kids jumping into a pool. Keep going until you have a pile of pages. Don't worry about having too many pictures. You can always review and edit before attaching everything to the board.

Step 3: Decide which quotes make it to the board. Maybe they all do.

Step 4: Place the fill-in-the-blanks on the board. You can use them as headings (if you want) and organize your images accordingly. Don't glue or tape anything down—yet. First, review the materials and then curate your selections, making sure that every image connects with your goals. Hold on to the extras for a future vision board.

Step 5: Glue everything on the board and post it in a hot spot. This could be above your bed, mirror, dresser, or anywhere that'll constantly remind you about your best self.

Step 6: Grab your cell phone and snap a picture of the board. This is the ultimate hot spot, because you'll carry that image with you.

Ready. Set. Go!

Your best-self collage is up! Good. Now comes the hard part. It's time to put everything into action. Try this three-part trick for boosting your confidence and moving out of your comfort zone.

Let's say your photography game is the business and your immediate goal is to become your school's official paparazzo, snapping pictures of games and parties. Sadly, no one knows about your incredible lens work and those photography classes you took over the summer except for your bestie.

First: Shake off the doubt. You've created a million reasons why they won't allow you to be the school's official student photographer. Push past it. Tell fear to have a seat, preferably somewhere in the nosebleed section of Michigan Stadium. **Second:** Hype yourself up. Think about all the reasons why you're the best person for the job and write it down. Nothing long and snooze worthy. Just three to five bullets points explaining your skills, experience, and ideas for improving the school's current photography situation. **Third:** Create a plan. Whip up a "Wow, you did that?" digital portfolio of your hottest flicks. Make it brief (eight to ten of your best shots), but power-ful. Mix up your pictures. Go for action, portrait, and candid shots.

Practice the main points with your bestie. Smooth out any kinks in your conversation, but most of all, remove any shaky treble from your voice. It's all about that bass. Arrange a meeting with someone in charge. On your big day, use those bullet points and digital photos to get the gig.

Here's a bonus trick: If you don't feel confident on the big day, pretend like you do. Who's going to know that you're acting? No one. (You already know your secret is safe with me.) Building confidence takes time, but when you make leaving your comfort zone part of your daily routine, like put-ting on socks before lacing up your kicks for gym class, believing in yourself gets easier to do. And unlike those trendy sneakers that've jogged more laps that you can remember in the gym, confidence will never go out of style. I promise.

Famous!

CHEAT SHEET NO. 1

I believe that I can:

_____

_____

_____

_____

I feel confident when I:

_____

_____

_____

_____

I hate hearing the word "no," but I won't let it break me because:

_____

_____

_____

_____

_____

2

THESE TROLLS AIN'T LOYAL

"My self-worth is not linked to your cruel words and actions. My self-esteem is not affected by your deliberate attempts to destroy my character. You have no power over me."

**—MARINA COHEN, *DEAR BULLY:*
*SEVENTY AUTHORS TELL THEIR STORIES***

Hollywood has tried to confuse us about trolls and their behavior for years. I point to *Frozen* and *The Lord of the Rings* trilogy as Exhibits A and B, respectively. In A, the beloved Disney flick, trolls are fat, inappropriate, and loud, but they mean well and may be a bit loving. But in B, the *Rings*, these trolls aren't the kind of creatures you invite over for Thanksgiving dinner and a slice of sweet potato pie. They're hideous beasts that are up to no good. In case you forgot, think about the cave troll who attacked Frodo and company in Moria in *The Fellowship of the Ring*... I thought that would jog your memory.

In real life, there isn't any confusion about social media trolls. They're the ones who post comments on Instagram photos, or wish you a slow, painful death on Yik Yak. That doesn't sound loving, does it? They crave attention and become energized when you take the bait and type a witty or equally hurtful comeback. Their mission is to hate on you and break you down, with the goal of making you stoop to their level. Remember the nursery rhyme "Sticks and stones will break your bones, but words will never harm you"? Don't believe it. That little tune was created way before the Internet, trolls, and cyberbullying became part of our daily lives. You know the drill: If words have the power to heal, then they most certainly have the power to harm you too.

This brings me to Kim Kardashian. I can't talk about trolls without mentioning her; it's impossible. She's worshipped and hated from both sides with equal amounts of energy, and has more than twenty-nine million followers on IG and more than thirty-one million on Twitter. If you know the Kardashian brand, then you already know the finer points of her IG timeline: red carpet moments, family time with her sisters, matching outfits with baby North, and anything she's promoting, like her cell phone ad or selfie book. Love or hate her, Kim knows the power of her popularity and is all about adding more zeros to her bank account. But have you ever stopped to read the comments posted on her timeline? One person went in about Kim's face, saying that she'd eventually look like her true self, "dog city." Ouch. The venom is real and unnecessary. Wouldn't it be better to avoid her IG and Twitter feeds than waste time insulting her?

Kim knows people attack her success, baby weight, booty, body, marriage, love-hate relationships with the media, etc. Sometimes she's silent and sometimes…she goes off on her critics, which is a no-no. Depending on who the celebrity is, their diehard fans—like Beyoncé's BeyHive, Rihanna's Navy, and Katy Perry's KatyCats—will do all the heavy lifting on social media so that the star doesn't even have to fire back, and we've all seen how messy that can be.

Other celebs or celeb offspring decide it's time to exit social media (temporarily or permanently), like actor/comedian Robin William's daughter, Zelda. In August 2014 Robin committed suicide by hanging, and days after his death some trolls tweeted Zelda Photoshopped images of her father's bruised neck. There were also awful comments like, "He did this to himself because of you." Death is hard enough for any family to deal with, but when people take extra steps to be hateful when someone is grieving, well, that kind of behavior is inexcusable.

The bullying pushed Zelda to cancel her account. She tweeted: "I'm sorry. I should've risen above. Deleting this from my devices for a good long time, maybe forever. Time will tell. Goodbye." People flooded her timelines with support and she thanked them by posting a Harvey Fierstein quote: "Never be bullied into silence. Never allow yourself to be made a victim. Accept no one's definition of your life; define yourself."

The Twitter police went after those trolls and suspended their accounts, but they probably popped up again with new identities. Sadly, it took Zelda's situation to push Twitter to improve their online abuse policies. We all know too many teens who've dealt with these cyberbullies in silence.

Hey! What Have I Ever Done To You?

Okay, I know what you're thinking: *I do have time to clap back at the nasty comments, plus I have a smart mouth and can deal with any heat that comes my way.* I'm not saying that you shouldn't stick up for yourself. Nor do I doubt that you're quick witted. (Hello, I am too!) But this isn't a fight worth winning. Don't acknowledge a troll's presence with a response. A wise person once said, "The moon doesn't bark at dogs." In case you didn't know it, you are the moon in that scenario. The other thing you shouldn't do is believe anything the trolls post about you. Don't let them into your head and don't wonder what others think of you, especially if your self-confidence is low or you suffer with depression. It's a trap.

Jessica Laney attended Fivay High School in Hudson, Florida, played soccer and, she was active on social media, including Tumblr. According to news reports, teachers said she was well liked and always smiling. What they didn't know was that Jessica was being bullied on Ask.fm. Instead of asking questions, kids posted comments like: "You have pretty eyes, but you're fat," and "Can you kill yourself already?" She sent a few upbeat responses, but it didn't stop. Reports say she closed her account twice and her friends begged her to stay off the site, but Jessica was curious about what people were saying about her. On the surface, it seemed like Jessica could handle the hate coming her way, but she couldn't. She killed herself. Her family, classmates, and teachers were devastated. There are too many stories about girls and boys like Jessica, who've been tortured via social media, email, and text message.

If you're being bullied online, you *aren't* helpless and you don't have to suffer in silence. Stopbullying.gov, endcyberbullying.org, and stompoutbullying.org have tips and suggestions to deal with trolls. Here's what I've learned from a few of these resources.

★★★ *Star Tips* ★★★

1. **Change your privacy settings:** If you're having a "Why didn't I think of that?" moment, you're not alone. The easiest way to keep the shenanigans to a minimum is to *control* who has access to you on social media. While having hundreds of followers is cool, you can feel a bit more secure knowing that you've approved all the folks in your space. It may be time to change your screen name and avatar too.

2. **Hit the block button:** I doubt we use this feature enough. Sometimes it's needed *after* you've selected all the people who are following you. If one or a few of them get out of pocket, don't engage in an empty back and forth. Exercise your right to remain drama free and block 'em.

3. **Gather evidence:** If there are too many humiliating posts on your timeline and your safety is threatened, take screenshots, print emails, put the messages in order by the date, and keep them as proof. You may need to show these emails or texts to parents and the police if the situation escalates from stupid insults to criminal behavior, like threats of violence and death, pornography, or hate speech.

4. **Get help:** When trolls are persistent and blocking them isn't enough—especially if they're stalking you and recording videos of you in private places, like the school bathroom—it's time to tell your parents and guidance counselor. Many schools have taken a serious stance against cyberbullying and have written specific consequences (suspension, anyone?) into their code of conduct. While bully prevention laws vary by state, most require schools to create policies to deal with traditional and electronic harassment—even if

doesn't happen on school grounds or property.

5. **Report it:** Most cell phone carriers and social media outlets have safety centers that outline inappropriate and appropriate behavior. And guess what? Cyberbullying often violates the term and conditions policy.

Trolling: Truth & Lies

Let's test how much you know about trolls and cyberbullies in the quiz below.

True or False

1. Cyberbullying is a harmless rite of passage. _____
2. Most teens ignore bullying on social media. _____
3. Close to fifty percent of teens who are bullied online delete their accounts. _____
4. Snapchat messages are gone forever. _____
5. It doesn't make sense to turn off the GPS or location feature of your phone. _____
6. Tracking a troll on an "anonymous" app will lead to a dead end. _____
7. Your cell phone company won't help teens who snitch on cyberbullies. _____
8. It's a good idea to save texts, chats, and posts from bullies. _____
9. Boys are more likely than girls to bully others online. _____
10. Student advisory boards always have a voice in their schools' anti-bullying programs. _____

Answers

1. False. Traditional bullying and cyberbullying can influence teens in different ways, but it's hardly harmless. According to nobullying.com, it can rob young people of their self-esteem and cause them to drop out of school, with some teens committing suicide.
2. True. Dosomething.org says ninety percent of teens who've seen bullying on social media ignore it.
3. True. In a 2014 McAfee survey, forty-seven percent of teens admitted to deleting their online accounts.
4. False. According to scopeproject.net, sometimes it's difficult to find a social media company's data retention info, but Snapchat retains logs of previous Snaps, including some unopened ones.
5. False. Leaving these functions on allows friends *and* strangers to see your location. Also, never post your home address online.
6. False. The best hacker will tell you that smartphones hold tons of personal info. Just because someone is anonymous on Ask.fm or Whisper, doesn't mean she (or he) can't be tracked down.
7. False. Most cell phone carriers have policies that punish cyberbullying.
8. True. Safekids.com says you may need these to prove when, where, how, and the length of time you were harassed, especially if there's a threat of violence.
9. False. Dosomething.org says girls are twice as likely as boys to be victims and perpetrators of cyberbullying.
10. False. School advisory boards don't always have a voice in these matters, but they should. It makes sense to include students, since they know which sites and apps teens use to bully one another. Cyberbullying.us says students can inform school officials about what they've seen online and suggest ways to handle attacks.

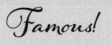

CHEAT SHEET NO. 2

I've decided to use my Instagram account to showcase my:

_____

_____

_____

_____

I'm not messing with these trolls because:

_____

_____

_____

_____

I'll change who can access my social media profile, if:

_____

_____

_____

_____

_____

3

CAUTION! YOU'LL BUMP YOUR HEAD AND SCRAPE YOUR KNEES LEAVING THIS PLACE

"Great people do things before they're ready. They do things before they know they can do it... Doing what you're afraid of, getting out of your comfort zone, taking risks like that—that's what life is. You might be really good. You might find out something about yourself that's really special and if you're not good, who cares? You tried something. Now you know something about yourself."

—AMY POEHLER

After completing a summer journalism workshop sponsored by the New York Association of Black Journalists for high school students at New York University, running around in trendy Greenwich Village in a NYU hoodie seemed all kinds of wonderful to me, but the school's price tag was pretty steep. And by pretty I mean ugly. Those zeros made me cringe. As a kid I was always painfully aware of how much things cost because my parents didn't speak the same money language. Ma was a coupon-clipping, spend-money-wisely-and-save-it-for-a-rainy-day person, while my entrepreneur Dad's vibe was you can't take it with you, so you might as well enjoy it. It was the best of both worlds. I learned to be brainy about money (hello, sexy savings!) from her and treat myself (hello, stylish shoes!) from him.

To prepare for college, Ma signed me up for the Brooklyn Alumnae Chapter of Delta Sigma Theta Sorority, Inc.'s Teen Lift program, which focused on understanding financial aid, writing a personal statement, college interviews, and visiting historically black colleges and universities (HBCUs). All I heard was *road trip*! I was always down to explore, even if it meant hours on a charter bus with cute boys. The moment we pulled into North Carolina with the Deltas, it was a wrap for attending school in NYC. Stepping onto that first tree-lined campus made me feel free. Do you know the beginning of *The Sound of Music* when Maria is spinning on the lawn and running around like it's her first time seeing grass? Well, that was me. And as it turned out, HBCUs were an affordable alternative, with many of them offering hefty scholarships to students with good grades and high SAT scores. Jackpot. I collected brochures for several universities and organized them based on size (small schools were most attractive to me), tuition, and their communication arts programs.

When we returned home, I researched more HBCUs. There were several popular schools like Howard, Hampton, and Spelman on my radar, but something about Johnson C. Smith University (JCSU) in Charlotte, North Carolina, spoke to me. I didn't tell Ma because she kept talking about NYC-based schools. The clock was ticking. Before I got up the nerve to say that I planned to attend JCSU in the fall, someone from the bursar's office called about the dorm deposit. Cue the scary music. Sitting on the edge of my bed, I chewed the inside of my cheeks. Ma stared at me as she talked to the bursar. "Where are you located?" she said. "Oh, North Carolina... I see." I wanted to sink into the mattress and disappear. You would've thought the school was on Pluto. What did she expect after sending me to Teen Lift? Did she think I was there just for the workshops? Nope! I was all about sleeping in a dorm room six hundred miles away from my family.

When she ended the call, I expected Ma to forbid me from going so far. I mean, it wasn't a few hours away, like Pennsylvania or Virginia. She played it cool. This wasn't her first rodeo with her independent thinking daughter.

"You don't know *anyone* in Charlotte, North Carolina," she said. This was absolutely true, and while I'd prepared my reasons why JCSU was the best choice for me and the family bank account, I didn't think knowing anyone was important. That was a small thing to a giant. Ma listened as I pleaded my case. I must've said something good because she wrote the check for the dorm fees, and in August, Dad packed up the minivan and we made the ten-hour trek to JCSU. Not being able to predict what would happen once my parents hit the interstate was the weirdest/best feeling *ever*. I was excited, curious, scared, and completely outside of my comfort zone (CZ), but I didn't care.

Wanna See A Magic Trick?

First, let me say that the CZ isn't a horrible place. It's a safe space to celebrate accomplishments and pat yourself on the back for something you already know how to do, which is fine for a temporary confidence boost, but it isn't a final destination. Think of it as a short layover between flights to becoming the star of your show. It's cozy, secure. But all that predictability makes you fearful to explore what's on the other side of the door. The most successful celebrities, athletes, techies, and business minds admit that the biggest rewards—what I like to think of as magic—happens when you step outside of those imaginary boundaries. Most of all, you'll inspire yourself and others (yes, other people are watching you) in the process. In my twisted mind, the CZ is flying overhead like a helicopter with a gang of hesitant jumpers inside. The altitude depends on the size of the opportunity placed in front of you. You have three options:

1. Stay inside, hold onto the railing and play it safe.
2. Grab your parachute and jump.
3. Get kicked out—without a parachute.

Confession: I've done all three at different times of my life. I learned nada about myself from playing it safe. On the flip side, my crash landings weren't cute either. Choosing JCSU was definitely a "grab a parachute and jump" moment that I don't regret. That experience shaped me and helped me land an important internship at *ESSENCE* magazine. My life would've looked much different without that first (and crucial!) media gig.

Things I've Done To Say Adiós To The CZ

1. Bought a ticket for one and watched a romantic comedy by myself.
2. Filmed a YouTube video.
3. Drove out of state by myself.
4. Wrote this book for you.
5. Chopped off my hair days before graduating from college.
6. Asked my crush to the prom. (He said no, but years later he asked me out. WINNING!)
7. Went to a party solo—and danced by myself.
8. Competed in a campus beauty pageant.
9. Agreed to be the keynote speaker at a girls' only conference.
10. Started a blog.
11. Performed a poem during an open-mic night.
12. Entered a short story contest. (I won second place.)
13. Went zip-lining in Jamaica.
14. Ran for senior class president in high school.
15. Baked a red velvet cake from scratch. (The icing was good, but the cake, uh, not so much.)
16. Raised a few thousand for my cousin Zae'Lyn's college fund.

Here's the part where I encourage you to get comfortable with being uncomfortable. I won't wave the do-something-that-scares-you-every-day flag, but two or three times a week will suffice and it doesn't have to be a major look. Well, maybe not in the beginning. There are items on my list that aren't newsworthy, but they're important to me. Driving out of state by myself was a huge personal accomplishment, because my sense of direction sucks and it's forced me to develop a deeply affectionate relationship with all five of my GPS apps. I'm totally cheating on them. Don't judge.

Oh, and I still crack up at my pictures from the campus beauty pageant as Miss Liston Hall. I represented the male freshmen dorm at JCSU. It was definitely an experimental period. While I adore sky-high heels, makeup, and cute haircuts now, it wasn't my thing back then and my pictures are proof of that! So before you decide to perform a one-woman play about Frida Kahlo's complex life, there are a few things you should know about leaving the CZ. Oh, just know I'm talking about taking healthy risks and goal setting here.

That bubbly feeling in your gut is fear: This isn't *Goldilocks and the*

Three Bears. That girl will get busted sleeping in Baby Bear's bed. That's fiction. This is nonfiction and you've entered choose-your-adventure mode. You don't know what the result will be, and you have to be cool with that. It's part of the process.

Everything won't be wrapped up pretty with a bow: Perfection is a myth, plus it's boring. Life gets messy. Be prepared to get dirty.

Get a co-conspirator: Connect with someone who knows a thing or two about a thing or two. If organizing a Women in Tech day in your community is too big a task to handle solo, get help from your squad or the girl with the solar-powered bedroom.

Change is a process, not an event: It's constant. Shoot a so-so YouTube video (like I did!), critique your work, and go back and shoot another one—minus the clunky parts.

Take baby steps: If the plan is to cook lamb chops with a balsamic reduction or herb crusted halibut but you've never boiled water for tea, then you need to start small. Master making a pot of brown rice and work your way up to a juicy piece a meat from there.

Realize that it's a crapshoot: This is the truth. You can screw up...or be totally amazing. There's only one way to find out.

Okay, Now It's Your Turn

Using my list as a guide, write down ten things you can do to leave the CZ. Side note: You may be naturally cautious or reserved and need to take more time leaving this comfortable place, which is cool. Don't rush before you're ready, but do commit to two actions per week. This is about exploration, like biking in a marathon or learning how to swim at the YMCA, not taking a harmful risk like rolling around naked in shards of glass. I don't see why anyone would *want* to do that but I had to bring it up, just in case you were curious about how far to take this whole thing.

The first action can be something as simple as buying one ticket to see that new action flick by yourself, or signing up to do The Color Run (also known as the Happiest 5K on the Planet). Be original. Grab a friend for support. Remember to write down how you felt before, during, and after the activity in your journal or on Post-it Notes you stick to your mirror. In two months, you'll become a pro at pushing yourself to try something new.

Things I'll Do To Leave The CZ

1. _____

2. _____

3. _____

4. _____

5. _____

6. _____

7. _____

8. _____

9. _____

10. _____

Go Cinderella

I gotta give it up to Keke Palmer. Her acting résumé zigzags all over the place, but in a good way. Most people remember her as the spelling whiz from *Akeelah & the Bee* or from her hit Nickelodeon show, *True Jackson, VP*. Although Keke has always been on my radar, from her stint on *90210* to *CrazySexyCool: The TLC Story* to *Abducted: The Carlina White Story*, she really made me say, "Hold up, wait a minute," with the *Just Keke* talk show. I mean, who does that? Most talk show hosts—Latifah, Ellen, and *The Real*'s Jeannie Mai—have more candles (read: age, wisdom, experience) on their birthday cake. But then I got it. Keke was the youngest talk show host in TV history, speaking directly to her peers while everybody else ignored them. Brilliant.

Then a few months later, Keke left her glass slipper on the staircase during her Broadway debut as Cinderella. Making the challenging leap from screen to stage was another huge moment. And as the first black woman to portray Cinderella, she remixed the classic fairy tale for so many girls who grew up seeing that character with blonde hair and blue eyes. After seeing Keke kill the leading role, I understood why she cried opening night. By leaving the CZ she'd changed the game for budding actresses—and herself—and little girls, like my niece Maya, who adore fairy tales.

One night, while starring in *Cinderella*, your girl Keeks couldn't sleep because she was criticizing and correcting her dance moves for an upcoming project, plus thinking about her matinee the next day and future acting gigs. Her mind wouldn't quiet down for a restful night's sleep and she posted this on IG: "When being all you can be is the goal... It isn't always comfortable."

I agree, Keke. Here's hoping fly girls like you never go back to the CZ.

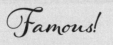

CHEAT SHEET NO. 3

It's time for me to leave my CZ because:

_____

_____

_____

_____

_____

The biggest challenge I have to leaving the CZ is:

_____

_____

_____

_____

When I accomplish my first major challenge, I will celebrate by:

_____

_____

_____

_____

Star Crush: **Mo'ne Davis**

If your brother says you throw like a girl, that's a compliment, especially if you know anything about Mo'ne Ikea Davis. This baseball player—whose arm is fifteen percent shorter than a major leaguer's—has a nasty set of limbs, and I mean that in the best way possible, because Mo mows down batters when she's at the mound. The average speed in this 14-year-old's age class is a high fifty mph, but she hurls a killer fastball at seventy mph.

This pitcher (who switched from softball to get down with the boys) was one of two girls in 2014's Little League World Series, and the first girl to win and pitch a shutout in Little League World Series history. If you're scratching your dandruff wondering about the significance of a shutout, it means Mo didn't let the opposing team score a run on her beloved Philadelphia Taney Dragons.

When the media caught wind of this honor student, every news outlet vied for a chance to hear her speak. Mo was interviewed everywhere from *CNN* to *The Tonight Show Starring Jimmy Fallon* to the *Steve Harvey Show*, and Spike Lee filmed a sixteen-minute documentary about the young woman who redefined the once hurtful jab "throw like a girl." First Lady Michelle Obama, Kevin Durant, Skylar Diggins, Ellen DeGeneres, and Magic Johnson all gave her shout outs on Twitter. *Sports Illustrated* blessed her with a cover shot—making her the first Little League baseball player to appear on the magazine—and Mo earned their SportsKid of the Year honor too. She also ended 2014 with the *Associated Press'* prestigious Female Athlete of the Year award. This kind of attention is wonderful and can cause anyone to get a big head, but what impressed Mark Bechtel, managing editor of *Sports Illustrated for Kids*, was her "poise and grace" under the spotlight, not just her accomplishments. One of the best results of her popularity is the influence she's having on girls and adults. She's become a role model with girls in the stands holding signs that read: "Show Me the Mo'ne," "I Wanna Throw like a Girl!" and "Go Mo!"

Six years before *Sports Illustrated* and the rest of the world took notice of Mo, Steve Bandura, who's a program director for the Marian Anderson Recreation Center in South Philly, saw her playing football with family members and throwing first-class spirals. Steve invited Mo to the center to watch the guys play basketball, but she wanted to run drills with them too. Later, she became his best player and the only girl on the team. Oh, and she excels at soccer too.

After watching Mo play, Pennsylvania governor Tom Corbett Jr. predicted that she'd play professional baseball someday. Tom Verducci of *Sports Illustrated* co-signed that statement, saying he could see a woman breaking into Major League Baseball in the pitcher position. That could be part of Mo's future, but for now, she has other plans. Her dream is to be point guard for the University of Connecticut's Huskies and hoop in the WNBA.

Last March we got a chance to read more about Mo's story in her book, *Mo'ne Davis: Remember My Name—My Story from First Pitch to Game Changer*.

4

DON'T BE AFRAID TO DEFINE
YOURSELF, FOR YOURSELF

"Part of the great challenge of living is defining yourself in your moment, of seizing the opportunities that you're given and of making the very best choices you can."

—HILLARY CLINTON

True story: Wendy Williams scared the crap out of me. You know how people's teeth chatter in below-zero temps? Well, imagine my bones underneath my skin, threatening to break loose. The best way to describe this is terror fabulous. It was a defining moment for me, and there was no way I'd allow nerves and a room full of people (more on that later) to have me looking crazy in these streets.

Let me explain. Wendy's TV show had just been picked up for a second season and I'd spent months emailing her publicist about an interview for *Juicy* magazine, but they weren't feeling me at all. I pushed until I got the green light; sometimes it's all about timing. I've chased actors, rappers, and reality stars, but this was the self-proclaimed Queen of All Media and the woman who'd earned the radio rep as the "biggest mouth in New York." I had to get Wendy. For me, part of the talk show host's appeal is her ability to dish about her flaws, including ex-boyfriends, miscarriages, and plastic surgery. "The warts," she later told me, "are part of what makes life fun."

Anyway, she was killing it in the top twenty markets alongside Ellen De-Generes and Rachael Ray. At her core, this big personality is just a Jersey girl from a solid middle-class family who did her thing on urban radio (with twelve million listeners) and parlayed her curiosity, tell-it-like-it-is advice into the talent and executive producer titles of the very successful, nationally syndicated gabfest known as *The Wendy Williams Show*. That's all, no biggie. Riiiiiight.

When I think about women who've defined themselves—without stopping to be distracted by a side eye, doubt, or shady comments—Wendy is in the top twenty of that list. Even if you're not a fan of her brand of entertainment, clap for her because she's never played sidekick Sally to a guy. She told an interesting story about this on mediabistro.com's *My First Big Break* video segment. It all started when she accepted a radio gig in St. Croix right after graduating from Northeastern University in Boston. This wasn't Wendy's dream job (or location) and she didn't tell friends about it because she knew people would try to talk her out of going. Wendy's plan was simple. She wouldn't fall in love or make friends (because hey, friends like to hang out and spend money) and her earnings were strictly for calling home to network with program directors. The future media player gave herself one year to leave St. Croix and return to the states. She beat her own deadline and left the U.S. Virgin Islands in eight months, and that's just one awesome tidbit from her backstory. There were more hurdles for Wendy to jump over throughout her career.

When personalities sit through back-to-back interviews, they become numb to the same list of questions from reporters, and they're human, so they get testy after a long day or call you out if you ask obvious or lazy questions. They can be mute, chatty, or pop off without warning. Within five minutes of the conversation, I usually know which switch to flip in my brain to make the most of the conversation. I hate canned answers, but I love, love, love when there's a moment of silence because I've asked something thought provoking.

My fear was that Wendy—who's known for snappy comebacks and for asking what everyone is thinking—would be bored, or say something like, "Is that all you got?" Her team asked for a list of questions and I submitted a few pretty generic ones (a trick of the trade), because I knew this was heading into don't ask this, don't ask that territory. They asked me not to talk to her about competition. Huh? Wendy is known for TMI, plus she left it all on the page in her memoir, *Wendy's Got the Heat.*

Grand ideas floated through my head about us sitting in her office chatting one-on-one about her show. Not so. The room was crowded with her makeup artist Merrell Hollis, *Juicy's* editor in chief Paula T. Renfroe, photographer Rayon Richards, and folks from Wendy's publicity team. Everybody had a job to do. Even Wendy's custom-made wigs sitting atop cute pink heads had a front-row seat to the interview.

Unsettling? Eh, yeah. But at least the wigs couldn't judge me. After months of convincing her people to let me in the studio, there was no way I'd allow multiple sets of curious eyeballs to mess with my head and screw up my moment. The only solution was to block 'em out. Good thing I did. The conversation flowed easily after she answered each question, and I completely forgot about terror fabulous and bones clinking loud enough to wake the dead. Wendy was super personable and approachable, and she dropped many jewels about career, success, and competition. Although there were other hosts vying for daytime viewers, Wendy decided a long time ago to be her own competition. That mission became her mantra. During her radio days she earned a place in the gossip game at a time when people were faxing—yep, this was pre-email and smartphone—hot tips about who was hooking up with whom. Today, *The Wendy Williams Show* airs in fifty-two countries and was renewed for its sixth, seventh, and eighth seasons.

Let's say it together in our Wendy Williams voice: "How you doin'?"

Where Does Your Book Begin?

So who are you? What are you? Which adjectives do you use to define yourself?

If your initial reaction is to grab a highlighter and mark up your flaws before somebody else does, don't do that. Everybody sees you with their own filter, so they may not even see your so-called imperfections. You know how it goes: A classmate compliments your *Grapes of Wrath* monologue and instead of being thankful, you point out where you forgot a few words. Your classmate had no idea. Instead of swirling around in that celebratory moment—which is just a snapshot of what you're really capable of—you smudge it with a mistake. Not cool. Start with the positive and continue to build from there. Maybe you saved a toddler from drowning last summer. Maybe you started a tutoring business for elementary school kids in your neighborhood. Maybe you go grocery shopping for the elderly woman in your building every week. This makes you a lifesaver, an entrepreneur, a volunteer. That's a way better story to tell than leading with a defect.

Back in the day I was so annoyed with my last name, even though it's a perfectly good adjective! From kindergarten to middle school, kids were thrilled when I gave the wrong answer in class, and the negative attention forced me to second-guess myself and pray to never get called on in math. That silent call for help went ignored. Sometimes I got it right and other times I botched multi-step linear equations. This led to being called Miss Not So Smart. Lucky for those people I don't hold grudges. (Side note: I don't believe in dumbing down for anyone. Beautiful minds deserve to be admired.)

I'm not alone. There was a great post on the photo blog Humans of New York (HONY), started by Brandon Stanton, about a girl who hates her name. I immediately related to her. I'm embarrassed to admit this, but...I hated my first name too because people mispronounced it all the freakin' time. I secretly wished it were Toya or Trisha. (I'm happy to report that I'm completely done with that phase. What you call me doesn't matter—but what I answer to does and Miss Dumb won't get a response.) But back to the girl on HONY, she said:

"Sometimes I hate my name because it always draws attention to me, and I'm not a very social person. My family moved this year from Pennsylvania. I was so scared the first day of school that someone would notice me. I wouldn't even adjust my seat because I thought it would make a noise. One time I really had to cough, but I held it in. When the teacher started calling attendance, I got really nervous, because every time people learn my name is Beyoncé, somebody starts singing 'Single Ladies.' And some did, of course. But the second day of school wasn't too bad. Because everyone knew my name."

The quote generated tons of responses on Facebook from other people who were bothered by their names at some point in their lives. More than twenty-two thousand people shared that FB post and more than three thousand liked it. People chimed in with their stories, including a woman named Holly Wood (dag, I feel for you, chica) and another named Summer Love. FB didn't believe Summer Love was a name, so she had to use a nickname instead. Then there were guys named Will Smith, Chris Brown, and Steve Madden. Sometimes parents just don't get it, huh? I never thought sharing a celebrity name had a downside, but it does. It can become the way people choose to define you, while the *real* you is overshadowed by the joke.

Names aside, people are quick to label others and put them in boxes, because it's easier to see someone via a limited filter—geek, thug, weirdo, jock, slut, bully, nerd, and the list goes on—than accept all of their amazing parts. One of my favorite authors, John Green (*The Fault in Our Stars*), who's definitely pro-nerd, flipped the word nerd into *nerdfighter*. He doesn't fight nerds, but in his world, a nerdfighter is made up of "awesome," rather than flesh and bone. Another bona fide brainiac, MSNBC political commentator Melissa Harris-Perry, embraced the word too, calling her show *nerdland* because she's all about smart discussions. Both Melissa and John reclaimed the word to give it power, so that it no longer stung and forced people to view them through a different lens.

Brave Starts Here

Often, we define ourselves by titles (Mostly Likely to Succeed), trendy possessions (iPhone 7) or physical build (chubby). But what if you couldn't rely on any of that? What if your physical appearance hid the champion underneath?

It took author, motivational speaker, and anti-bullying activist Lizzie Velasquez a minute to discover her purpose. Born with a rare disease (only two other people in the world have it) that left her blind in one eye and doesn't allow her to gain weight, she wasn't expected to talk or walk. For those of us with an addiction to kettle-cooked chips and chocolate bars, the no-weight-gain aspect sounds all kinds of amazing. Lizzie even jokes about it during her incredible TEDxAustinWomen talk. She's learned to make light of the situation, but on the serious tip, she gets sick often and has never weighed more than sixty-four pounds. For a long time, Lizzie allowed her outside—skinny arms and legs—to define who and what she was, until one video changed everything.

You've probably heard about Lizzie from "The World's Ugliest Woman" video. Someone took an eight-second piece of an interview she'd done with a local television station, posted it to YouTube and gave it that heartbreaking title. Lizzie was a high school student when she found the video while searching for music online. The infamous clip racked up four million views and comments that labeled her a monster and suggested: "Put a gun to your head and kill yourself."

Lizzie was devastated. She later told *Fox News Latino* that her parents allowed her to have one "good cry" to get all of her feelings out, then encouraged her to move onto something positive. With her family's support, Lizzie figured out a way to take charge of how things played out. While the "kill it with fire" comments hurt, she couldn't—and wouldn't—let them crush her spirit. Lizzie fought back by allowing her accomplishments to outshine her condition. Her strategy was to become a college graduate, author, and motivational speaker. She's done all of this and starred in a documentary, *A Brave Heart: The Lizzie Velasquez Story*, about her anti-bullying crusade. It premiered at SXSW 2015 and the tagline focuses the lens on how people should see Lizzie, saying: "Bullying stories are famous for having victims, not heroes." As I watched the trailer, all I could think was if Lizzie found the strength to define herself, the challenge is so much easier for those of us *without* a rare condition. Using Lizzie's life as an example, here are some dos and don'ts to help identify the real you.

★★★ *Star Tips* ★★★

Do

1. Think beyond the superficial: Selfies have turned our nation's fixation on looks into a full-time job. Everyone is after the right angle or app to appear slim and pretty, but beauty changes (and it doesn't just belong to young people) so avoid making that your sole descriptor. And I hate to break it to you, but there will always be someone who's prettier, skinnier, and/or curvier than you. Trust.

2. **Recognize your gifts and celebrate them:** Can you memorize a script quickly? Are you an excellent writer? Can you play music by ear? Do you make people laugh? Can you skate a perfect figure eight? These may seem like minor gifts, but they're actually what make you special. If you're stumped, check out the Bragging Rights activity to jumpstart your personal celebration.

3. **Rewrite the scene:** Stumbling across that ugly woman clip was a turning point for Lizzie. Motivated by being bullied online, Lizzie authored three books, including *Be Beautiful, Be You*, and *Choosing Happiness*, and speaks to everybody from corporate execs to students about overcoming obstacles.

Don't

1. **Define yourself by what you abhor:** That list can get pretty exhausting, especially since social media has turned hate into a blood sport. Focus on what brings you joy, where you excel, or where you'd like to improve.

2. **Co-sign labels from others:** Labels, even seemingly harmless ones, can limit the way you see yourself. Often it's a limited way of thinking too.

3. **Stop rewriting the script:** As you grow and learn more about yourself, you're going to need additional notebooks for those accomplishments, big and small. Avoid falling into just one way of seeing yourself. You're free to change your mind. Hey, in the fifth grade I thought I would be known for winning the Olympic gold medal in double Dutch. It didn't take long to nix that idea...

Who Am I?

The dictionary defines words so that we understand meaning, parts of speech (noun, verb, adjective etc.), and how to pronounce them correctly. In life, you create a personal dictionary and write the story of how you want to be portrayed based on your actions. Lizzie Velasquez and Wendy Williams defined themselves based on goals, circumstances, and the mark they wanted to leave on the world.

There are different triumphs and challenges along the way for both women—remember how Twitter came for Lifetime's *Aaliyah: Princess of R&B* biopic? They tore into everything about it from the casting to the script, which was executive produced by Wendy. But the TV host, who's quite familiar with unfriendly fire, responded in classic form during a Hot Topics segment on her own show. She said: "I see my Aaliyah movie broke the Internet this weekend! Errbody got an opinion. Well, I must tell you, whether you loved or hated it, you watched. It was the second-highest rated movie on all of cable this year so far." Did people really expect Wendy to melt like cheese on toast from all the heat being tossed at her flick? Uh, hello, that's not the way she's built. That's not to say she didn't secretly fume about the tweets and wish for critical acclaim in private. But in public? Nah, that's not even in her style. That's not how she writes *her* story.

So here's your challenge. Answer this question: **Who am I?** This isn't about how others see you. It's about how you see you—without any filters (you know how we love those on IG) and without worrying about what your parents, your boo, or your best friends are going to think. Use adjectives. (Sometimes I'm quirky. Thoughtful. Funny. Generous. Selfish. Selfless.) Think about how you react when life is tossing you lemons—and you want to make lemonade, but really you don't want no stinkin' lemonade. Don't edit yourself. Take a moment to celebrate your accomplishments. Write down why you love yourself. Think about you've changed in the last year, or how you handled a life-changing situation, like moving to a new city or dealing with your mom getting remarried. Be honest about what's important to you and why.

I am:

_____

_____

_____

_____

_____

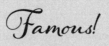

CHEAT SHEET NO. 4

I'll celebrate my gifts because:

_____

_____

_____

_____

I don't co-sign labels from others because:

_____

_____

_____

_____

From now on I'll define myself by:

_____

_____

_____

_____

_____

_____

_____

5

EVERYBODY NEEDS A FAVE FIVE

"Everyone wants to ride with you in the limo, but what you want is someone who will take the bus with you when the limo breaks down."

—OPRAH WINFREY

A peek inside my brain would reveal a box of movie tickets, passages from books, a half-eaten sandwich, warm memories of baby sister Anika, scrap paper with interesting doodles, and a good pen. I sketch problems, solutions, stories, and scripts as part of my thought process, but not as well as Jessica Hagy, the artist and writer behind the super smart blog thisisindexed. com, and author of *How to Be Interesting in Ten Simple Steps*. (I heart this book because she emphasizes that leaving a mark is greater than leaving a blemish. A simple yet effective message. Man, it doesn't get better than that.)

I checked out Jessica's work and she earned a spot on my ever-growing crush list (she's in good company), because she uses "visuals to tell stories, jokes and truths." We've never met, but she does follow me on Twitter (hey, girl, hey!), so that makes her the long-distance homie in my mind. Anyway, Jessica penned this dope post on forbes.com about "The Six People You Need In Your Corner"; they include The Task Master, who demands that you get stuff done, and The Doubter, who asks the tough questions. I was immediately hooked on this idea that none of us survive our big, fat juicy mistakes and get to Awesomeville without a real ride-or-die crew. For the record, the fake ones wanna be down *after* you become successful. As Rick Ross said: "You wasn't with me shooting in the gym." Look around. Who's been pushing you to be your best?

Inspired by Jessie's list (maybe she'll let me call her this when we meet), I've whipped up a remix for you called the Fave Five. In business, the FF or Six People are considered your board of directors. They're a body of elected/ appointed peeps that collectively oversee a company or organization so that things don't break faster than a pair of sunglasses you accidentally sat on. Having them in your corner is a no-brainer, especially since you're a newbie seeking real-world experience. You have questions and they have answers. You have problems and they have solutions.

I hate to break it to you, but this group of guys and gals isn't comprised of your BFFs. Those peeps roll in their own, special lane in your life, but we're discussing one that is above their pay grade. Unless they are super qualified, none of your friends are part of your Fave Five. I'm so serious. You need folks who are seasoned, i.e. people who have actually lived a little, been tossed around by life, failed and succeeded and bought the T-shirt. At least one of them has earned a reserved spot in the limo when you go big time. And because she's patient, believes in you, and understands that the universe won't be rushed, she carries bus fare for the both of you—just in case it takes three years vs. three months for your Big Idea to pop off.

Where do you find these special people for your list? They're right in front of you, being underutilized. They know your goals, know where you're headed, and can motivate you to keep on moving. They're (adult) friends and family who fit into the go-getta column. So your ol' camp counselor who started a nonprofit to empower teen boys qualifies, as does your aunt who hosts cool events like swimming in the San Francisco Bay to raise money for her favorite charity.

Without further ado, let me introduce you to your Fave Five.

Code Name: **The Social Butterfly**
Specialty: **Making Introductions**

She's mad mixxy, attending everything from a Detroit Lions football game to a museum opening to an exclusive Sunday brunch with members of the city council. The Social Butterfly air-kisses the cheeks of royalty, but more important, she's friendly with the gatekeepers too. This means she can get your résumé to the right people for that important first internship, or even set up a time for you to shadow a power player.

Code Name: **The Deadline Diva**
Specialty: **Tough-Love Reminders**

This one lives by her calendar and is all about sending reminders so that there aren't any excuses, only results. If your application to a summer arts program is due in two weeks, expect The Deadline Diva to call five days early to hit send on the electronic form. She's constantly checking in—which can be annoying—but it's all out of love, because she understands that time is an undervalued commodity.

Code Name: **The Coach**
Specialty: **Focused On Solutions**

She has the popcorn and juice ready for a strategy session to launch your graphic design business. The Coach listens intently to uncover holes in your blueprint and pushes you to find solutions. For example, if your current computer is on life support, she'll ask: when can you get a new one, and do your parents have the funds to buy it? Can you offer to pay half of the bill with that birthday stash tucked away in your dresser? Don't think about wasting her time, either. Come prepared with a list of questions and be ready to execute at least two of her suggestions.

Code Name: **The Treasurer**
Specialty: **Investing Time And Money**

Sometimes it comes down to needing a few extra dollars for that senior trip, or additional cash to buy supplies for your budding cupcake business when unexpected orders roll in. She understands that eight dozen sweet treats for a kids' birthday party is a good problem. No matter what, The Treasurer, who saves more than she spends, admires your hustle and considers you a worthwhile investment. However, don't abuse her kindness, or treat her like your personal ATM.

Code Name: **The Seer**
Specialty: **Enhanced Vision**

She doesn't possess a crystal ball, a third eye, or tarot cards, but she's definitely all knowing. The Seer is a fan, but she isn't about blind worship. She knows that you're capable of organizing and raising serious cash at the basketball fund-raiser, so her advice is useful and practical. She also zooms in on the details, like reminding you to ask parents to sign photo and video release forms for their kids before game day.

It's Time To Recruit Your Team

There isn't a hard and fast rule for selecting your Fave Five. Maybe you should replace The Deadline Diva with The Role Model because the latter team member is currently living in NYC, which is your dream city or has your dream job as a veterinarian. That's cool. This doesn't need a formal announcement.

For example, with The Social Butterfly, call her up or send an email (depending on how close you are) and thank her for inviting you to the mayor's scholarship dinner. Compliment her work and ask if it's okay for you to connect with her when you need advice and support. Remember to come bearing gifts. It's the polite thing to do and shows that you care about more than just yourself. After all, this can't be a one-way relationship where you suck The Social Butterfly dry. If you know she loves Starbucks' Pike Place coffee, buy a bag as a thank-you. If you're a DIY girl, create a bracelet that includes her initials. A gift doesn't have to break the bank, but it *must* be thoughtful. Former intern Donovan Moore once brought cookies to one of our meetings—simply because he knows I love snacks. Smart! Oh, and don't only connect with them when you need something. Remember to text, email, Skype, or send cards with good news or during the holidays.

Now it's your turn. Decide how to fill up your Fave Five draft card. Which adults can share information, help make a connection, hold you accountable, and support your goals? Make a list of at least ten people, then edit it down to the core group that you can really depend on when it's crunch time.

My Fave Five:

1. _____

2. _____

3. _____

4. _____

5. _____

Okay, your team is ready. Fill out their code names and specialties. Feel free to use the names provided here or remix as many of the categories as you wish to match your situation (i.e. swap The Deadline Diva with The Role Model).

Code Names And Specialties

Code Name: _____

Specialty: _____

What She/He Does: _____

Code Name: _____

Specialty: _____

What She/He Does: _____

Code Name: _____

Specialty: _____

Famous!

What She/He Does: _____

Code Name: _____

Specialty: _____

What She/He Does: _____

Code Name: _____

Specialty: _____

What She/He Does: _____

Four Friends Every Girl Needs

Before you think that I shaded your besties with that "above their pay grade" comment, know that wasn't my intention at all. So there's no need for the side eye. Best friends play a valuable role in your day-to-day existence that the Fave Five are clueless about. You need both groups, they just drive in different lanes.

For the record, Mindy Kaling, creator and star of *The Mindy Project*, is my bestie in my head, but if we knew each other (I mean, other than me stalking her timeline, watching her shows on repeat, and reading her books) we'd be tighter than a fresh pair of Spanx. I just know it. I'd probably add her to my Fave Five list too, because I see the benefit of having a smart, funny, creative woman with Hollywood bank on my team. Below are a list of four friends you should have—and ways they can make you a better person.

The Ambitious One: She's focused on her focus and doesn't allow slackers in her circle. This friend brings home a near perfect GPA every semester—even with an afterschool job at Michaels. She's the first student teachers recommend for awards, scholarships, and special programs, but she isn't their pet. **Why you need her:** She motivates you to push harder and do more with your twenty-four hours. Plus she co-signs your dreams about becoming a pediatrician, while everyone else says it's out of your reach.

The Divergent One: Under normal circumstances, this girl wouldn't be on your radar, but your dads are friends, so you were forced to be together on many occasions and your relationship grew from there. You don't share similar interests in music, movies, or games, but that's okay because you secretly envy that she's outspoken, passionate, and doesn't color inside the lines. **Why you need her:** She sees the world through a totally different lens, which inspires you to tap into your serious side, or donate your birthday money to a charity instead of blowing money fast at the mall.

The Creative One: She's gifted in various areas—drawing, singing, acting, and painting—while others struggle to find their one true talent. Her art is always beautiful, even when she's spotlighting something painful, like her little brother's illness. **Why you need her:** She encourages you to use art to express yourself and you enjoy attacking a canvas with a paintbrush for an abstract piece, instead of keeping those emotions bottled up.

The Funny One: She's smart and makes you laugh in the middle of the crazies without even trying. She's quick to poke fun at herself before taking a hurtful swipe at others, but beware when she does—her wit cuts deeper than a razor. **Why you need her:** She's the perfect person to hook up with after midterms or final exams, or even a failing grade in humanities. Her rendition of Juliet breaking up with Romeo is Masterpiece Theater, and quiet as kept, she can tutor you in several subjects.

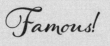

Famous!

CHEAT SHEET NO. 5

My Fave Five is everything because:

_____

_____

_____

_____

I've added a sixth person to my squad because:

_____

_____

_____

_____

The first challenge one of my Fave Five can help me with is:

_____

_____

_____

_____

_____

_____

6

DON'T MAKE THEM CALL THE FASHION POLICE

"Clothing is ultimately the suit of armor in which we battle the world."

—SOPHIA AMORUSO

In high school, I wasn't anyone's fashion plate. Nor was I eligible for the *Fashion Police*'s worst dressed list. At least I don't think I was, but the photos in my shoebox probably tell a different story. One thing is clear: I had a good time experimenting with different looks until I found one that stuck, and even that was a temporary situation because I remixed things again in college. Like you, my clothes reflected my mood or whatever held my interest at that moment.

There was the designer phase, which ended before it even started because: 1) I was following what everyone else was into (which didn't work for me then or now), 2) I didn't have the cash flow to buy anything by anybody named Gucci or Louis (and even an afterschool job wouldn't cover all the zeros for those labels), and 3) my parents refused to support my shenanigans with their hard-earned coin. The club kid moment allowed me to channel my inner weirdo and wear bright yellow pants, fedoras, black turtlenecks, and maroon suspenders. Then there was the Afrocentric period with kente cloth, Africa medallions, and large crowns (hats). After that I entered young CEO mode, wearing blazers and carrying a briefcase.

Where do most people get their style inspiration? Celebrities or characters, right? I wasn't any different. At one point I took my cues from *The Cosby Show*'s Clair Huxtable and my nickname became Ms. Huxtable. This gorgeous wife and mother of five was an attorney who was devoted to her family and career. Although I didn't have any interest in law, I was sold on her business look. Plus, I landed a job with the IRS via the Summer Youth Employment Program. When I dressed like Clair Huxtable, they treated me like a young adult instead of some high school kid who sucked up oxygen and took up valuable office space during the summer.

Sadly, all of my summer and part-time jobs weren't as cushy as the one at the IRS. I had one retail gig at a discount clothing store that shall remain nameless, which helped me realize that this girl wasn't built to fetch cheap tank tops for rude customers. Not that I could afford to stick my nose up at any job with a paycheck attached. While my parents never pushed me to find an afterschool job or part-time situations, I pressured myself to make my own coin. Ma always said: "Your job is to get good grades." Well, those As and Bs weren't paying for any new blazers or hanging out with my friends.

Here's the thing about the Golden Rule: She (or he) who has the gold— rules. There were clothes Ma refused to buy simply because the price tag sent her into sticker shock. I thought she was being stingy, but once I had my minimum-wage paycheck in hand I understood—and learned how—to make a dollar holler. Everything above my pay grade stopped being a must-have item if *I* had to pay for it. Money meant freedom and the chance to splurge on baked ziti during fake power lunches at Sbarro. (If I'd known I'd become lactose intolerant later in life, I would've savored those delicious chunks of mozzarella cheese a lot more.) Maybe dressing like Clair attracted a fair share of chuckles, but it was my thing at the time and at least I knew how to dress for a job interview—and looking the part was just half the battle.

These days you'll find millennial millionaires running companies in hoodies and jeans, but that doesn't mean you can show up to an interview looking like that. They've earned that right. Look professional, show them you mean business, get the job, and then adopt the office dress code.

Interview Clothes 101

Plain Pullover

Why you need it: Because that "I Am Hip-Hop" graphic tee isn't appropriate for every occasion. If blouses and button-up shirts aren't your thing, a fresh scoop or V-neck will beat a raggedy tee any day. **Suggestions:** White or black works well under a black blazer and it doesn't make you look stuffy or, worse, like you're trying too hard. Go for a pop of color like red, pink, or yellow. Bright hues make me happy like Pharrell. For proof, check the book cover. I'm giving you all kinds of sunshine.

Black Blazer

Why you need it: It goes with everything. It's what the magazines call a must-have staple for your closet—a classic, if you will. **Suggestions:** Cop a boyfriend blazer because you'll feel more comfortable and you won't look like you borrowed one of your mom's super corporate pieces. These days it's easy to find one everywhere, from H&M to Topshop. Pair it with a bright-colored pullover, blouse, or button up and you'll be unforgettable.

Simple Earrings

Why you need it: Accessories add polish to any outfit and take your white V-neck and black blazer combo up a few notches. **Suggestions:** Studs or small hoops. Plain ones are always safe, or opt for something sparkly in the center of the stud. Pick your pleasure, but remember the person should be focused on your face, not distracted by ten-inch chandeliers. I'm partial to hoops because I have a short haircut. I love big, gold (well, gold-plated because I also lose things) earrings the size of my head, but I know when to reel it in and look like I'm going to a scholarship dinner vs. a Kendrick Lamar concert in Prospect Park.

Ballet Flats

Why you need it: Heels aren't for everybody and the most beautiful ones will make your little piggies cry "wee, wee, wee" all the way home. So when you can't wear sneakers (even if they have a cute wedge like my green Nike Dunks) and heels aren't your thing, flats are a stylish alternative. **Suggestions:** In terms of color options, basic black or nude is always good, but trust the fashionistas who swear gold, silver, and leopard are neutral enough to go with everything.

Bras That Fit

Why you need it: The experts say eighty percent of women wear the wrong bra size. So if you haven't had your breasts measured in a while (or ever), it's safe to assume that you're part of that club. I've been there too. Recently I had that whole third boob situation happening and it wasn't cute. (That's when your bra doesn't fit and "the girls" are jammed together, making it look like baby triplets are fighting in your T-shirt.) The goal here is to minimize the jiggle and support your breasts to prevent injury, especially when you're chasing a soccer ball down the field or hurling a baseball toward second base. **Suggestions:** Get your lady parts measured at a department store or specialty shop. The bra specialists at Victoria's Secret have hooked me up plenty of times. Just know this isn't a one-and-done deal. You're still growing, so your breasts will continue to change shape and size. They're also a different size during your menstrual cycle, and if you're super normal, like me, one of your boobs is bigger than the other. But that's our little secret.

Extra Goodies

Fashion tape: This double-sided treasure used to be a celebrity secret (yep, we're on to you, Miss Ariana Grande), but now it's right there for the rest of us at the checkout line at Old Navy. Use it to keep bra straps in place or fix a fallen hemline without a needle and thread.

Stain Remover: Ah, the messy girl's best friend can be scooped up from Wal-Mart. Use your favorite brand on fresh stains like ketchup, tea, barbecue sauce, and food; it won't work on a four-month-old chocolate syrup blob, sorry.

Blouse Button (formerly known as the Bosom Button): When you've realized that one of your buttons has escaped from Fabric Town, or there's a gap that leaves your bra exposed, this is a waaaay better option than a safety pin.

The buttons come in round or square shapes and in black, rose, crystal, and more. Check 'em out at blousebutton.com.

★★★ *Star Tips* ★★★

Some Basic—but Extremely Important—Dos

1. **Wear a blazer:** I mentioned this earlier and if you have one, great. There's something about a blazer that says you mean business. People take you more seriously. Maybe you don't have all the qualifications necessary to work the cash register at The Container Store and the guy next to you has four years of experience, but he's wearing a wrinkled T-shirt with a mustard stain on it. If I were responsible for hiring the cashier, I'd choose you. Personal appearance is critical, and the person ringing up customers should always look pulled together, not like she rolled out of bed and spilled condiments on her clothes before heading to work.

2. **Think Triple C:** If you don't have a blazer, don't have the cash to buy one, and borrowing one is out of the question, go for Triple C, i.e. a crisp, clean collar. Grab the spray starch, iron one of your favorite button-up shirts, and pair it with a skirt or pants. Khakis are cool and plain, black jeans are a decent substitute for black pants. And if you are interviewing at Target, those khakis will come in handy.

3. **Get a second opinion:** Check in with someone whose knows a lil' somethin' somethin' about job interviews to chime in on your outfit, nails, hair, and makeup. Don't fly into an obnoxious rage if your big sister says kill the miniskirt and the thigh-high boots. She's right. Skirts should hit the knee. Keep in mind that you're interviewing for a job at Staples, not to replace a member of Fifth Harmony.

4. **Schedule a dress rehearsal:** A few days before the interview, put on the entire outfit and walk around the house. Stand up and sit down. This may sound extra, but there's nothing like finding out your foot grew a half-size

hours before the interview—and you don't have an extra pair of shoes. This gives you time to fix any wardrobe malfunctions. Stand in front of the mirror and give yourself a once-over. You should look and feel comfortable. This will save you time and prevent frustration. How do I know? I've had plenty of zippers break before a big fund-raiser, wedding, or graduation. What can I say? Sometimes the fashion gods are just cruel to me, but those experiences taught me to test the outfit and *always* have a backup.

5. **Keep it simple:** Pastel blue hair, septum rings, and unicorn heads on acrylic nails are doing the most in an accounting office, but may be creative and cool in a thrift store. As I've mentioned, dressing the part is key. I worked with a guy who appeared to be very conservative. But it wasn't until he rocked shorts at a barbecue that I saw his legs were covered in tattoos. Turns out he chopped off his ponytail, chucked his earrings, and covered his tats to land a nonprofit gig. My dude was hardly conservative, but he dressed like everyone else to get the job. Full disclosure: I've had blue hair and a fauxhawk (a fake Mohawk) at different times in my life. In creative (and tech) environments the rules are quite relaxed, but please know that if Anna Wintour called with a gig at *Vogue*, I would've dyed my hair black before the interview. I saw *The Devil Wears Prada* and I know you did too.

6. **Go easy on the makeup:** Ever heard of the saying, "Less is more"? Yeah, that goes double here. Leave the paint box exploration for the weekends. Now is not the time for glitter eyelids, crunchy eyelashes, rainbow nails, and Manic Panic's After Midnight Blue Lethal Lipstick. That shade is fun and I'm completely jealous of girls who can pull it off, but leave it for the weekend.

Oh, One More Thing

Sooooo, the following info has absolutely nothing to do with clothes, but they're life lessons that are super important to the interview process. I know this chapter is about your dress code, but what good is having the right outfit if your résumé is jacked up?

Print extra copies of your résumé: Although you've submitted an application online and attached your résumé, put three extra copies in a folder and take it with you.

Chances are the interviewer:

1.   Didn't read your res
2.   Read it, but your name doesn't ring any bells
3.   Forgot to grab a copy for the meeting

If/when the manager asks for your résumé, you'll be prepared and ready to answer questions instead of wondering if this mistake will count against you or makes you look unprepared. Make sure that document is flawless, i.e. no typos, grammatical errors, or spaghetti sauce stains from last night's dinner. Get another set of trusted eyes to proofread it. Also, research the store, company, or organization with which you're interviewing. Know at least three facts that you can plug into the conversation. This info can help you shine bright during a meeting or save you if the conversation is going downhill faster than Lindsey Vonn on a set of skis. For her that's a good thing; for you, not so much.

Let's say you're interviewing at a big box store. Check their corporate website to discover some good nuggets about the company. Do they give back to the community and if so, how? Obvi, you don't drop this jewel at random, but when the conversation requires a bit of Big Box IQ, use it to impress the person sitting across from you with the twenty questions.

And...

Show up to the interview solo: You aren't Nicki Minaj. There's no need for Meek Mill and his entourage to come with you. Go ahead and tell the Drake wannabes to fall back. Bringing friends to an interview is unprofessional. If you need support, they can send good vibes from the 7-Eleven down the block, but no one should see them with you. There was a college freshman who applied for an internship at *Juicy* magazine and she looked fantastic on paper. Naturally, I was excited to meet and hire her if she aced the interview. In person, she gave so-so answers, failed to research the mag, and showed up with her relative who had a stink attitude. Her stock plummeted the moment she opened the glass doors with her cousin, who plopped down on the couch and asked: "Is this going to take long?" No, that interview didn't take long at all. I was eager to move onto the next candidate, who killed it and got the job.

#OOTD Challenge...Well, Sorta

If the interviewer is more than four years older than you, she (or he) may be secretly giving you the side eye. People give you the once-over and make assumptions from the moment you leave your house. Everything is judged (from chipped nail polish to a linty hoodie) all before the "hellos" and "pleased to meet yous" are said. That's why your interview outfit is so important. It's time to put what you've learned into practice.

Here's the scenario: You've filled out apps everywhere and the local children's museum, the new sneaker store in the mall, and a local medical center want to meet you Tuesday, Wednesday, and Thursday. Open your closet and create three head-to-toe interview outfits. Put them on and snap a full-length selfie in each outfit and send the images to one of your Favorite Five for feedback. By the end of this exercise you'll have a few go-to appropriate outfits ready, so you don't even have to think about what to wear when those calls start rolling in.

She (or he) must:

1. Provide feedback
2. Offer suggestions for the remix (i.e. ways to improve the outfit)
3. Give an overall rating on a scale of one to five, five being the highest

First Outfit

Top: _____

Bottom: _____

Shoes: _____

Accessories: _____

Feedback

_____

_____

Rating: _____

Second Outfit

Top: _____

Bottom: _____

Shoes: _____

Accessories: _____

Feedback

_____

_____

Rating: _____

Third Outfit

Top: _____

Bottom: _____

Shoes: _____

Accessories: _____

Feedback

_____

_____

Rating: _____

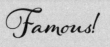

CHEAT SHEET NO. 6

I'm an excellent candidate for this job because:

_____

_____

_____

_____

_____

My best traits are:

_____

_____

_____

_____

_____

If I had a difficult time with a co-worker I'd:

_____

_____

_____

_____

_____

Star Crush: **Sophie Umazi Mvurya**

Peace is such a small word with huge definition. It's a state of being, according to *Merriam-Webster*'s dictionary. Yet it can also be a movement if helmed by the right person—a person like Sophie Umazi Mvurya, a young woman who fought against senseless killings and violence in Kenya.

From 2007 to 2008, Kenya experienced turmoil triggered by its controversial presidential election. One man was sworn in at the state's capitol, while another claimed victory. Everyone was confused and it appeared that the election was rigged. This sparked fifty-eight days of post-election violence, leaving more than one thousand people dead and six hundred thousand civilians displaced.

Sophie was almost killed in the madness. Three men thought she was from an enemy tribe because her skin is much fairer than most Kenyans. She was frightened, of course, but also furious that these men hated her simply because of her complexion, something she couldn't control. In her TEDxTeen talk, "Picture This Peace," Sophie explained that she was able to buy her way out unharmed. She doesn't know where she found the words to escape that situation "alive and breathing" and without any bruises, only that her quick thinking saved her life.

In 2012, while at the African Leadership Academy in South Africa, Sophie read that Kenya might experience another wave of election violence. She knew she had to do something to promote cultural understanding and encourage citizens of the world to support her country. Inspired by French photographer JR's Inside Out global art project, Sophie launched I AM KENYAN. Like Inside Out, IAK used photos to promote peace during the 2013 elections. She encouraged people to take a picture of themselves with the tag I AM KENYAN. This was significant for people in her country who were used to identifying themselves by a specific ethnic tribe, like Bantu, Nilotic, or Cushite. In four days, Sophie's efforts reached four thousand people and garnered eighty-five photos from twenty countries. A movement was born.

Six months after the program launched, IAK, with the help of social media, received ten thousand photos from couples, children, a former police spokesman, and even the former vice president of Kenya. Images poured in from all over the world, including Europe and America, along with thirty thousand peace signatures. The pictures were used in TV ads and blown up to poster size for billboards and various events around the country. Today, Sophie can count more than just images as part of IAK's success. The movement includes peace marathons, rugby, and soccer matches. Sophie, now a student at Oberlin College and owner and designer of Umazi Fashion, continually works to rebrand the image of her country via Kenyan-based fashion shows and cultural galleries.

And what happened during the 2013 elections? It was peaceful and there was an eighty-eight percent voter turnout, which was the highest Africa had ever seen. Since then, more than twenty-one thousand people around the world took pictures (with an outreach of eight million) and uploaded them on the group's site and Facebook page with the supportive caption: I AM KENYAN.

Peace was abruptly disturbed in 2015 when a group known as the al-Shabaab (from nearby Somalia) stormed the Garissa University College campus, armed with guns and grenades, and killed 147 people, mostly students. Still, the I AM KENYAN movement continues to grow. The spark has been lit for peace, and activists like Sophie continue to keep it burning.

7

PERMISSION GRANTED: CHOOSE YOUR OWN ADVENTURE

"I haven't been everywhere, but it's on my list."

—SUSAN SONTAG

In 1999's sci-fi film *The Matrix*, Neo (a.k.a. The One) is faced with a serious decision. Morpheus, his mentor, waxes poetic about how we're all born into a mind prison but we're not enlightened enough to know it. The scene is ultra dramatic: Morpheus speaks in a cadence that makes every sentence seem like a life or death matter, while Neo stares with puppy-dog eyes, eagerly soaking up his advisor's wisdom. You remember the blue pill/red pill speech: Does Neo choose to continue life in ignorance, or does he want to know his reality? Spoiler alert: Neo grabs the crimson capsule—choosing the truth—and chases it with a sip of water.

Ah, such is life. It's a series of decisions, large and small, with the potential to "send you down the rabbit hole" to find Neo looking all cool dressed in black leather. Online, the sci-fi and *Matrix* geeks (I say that with love from one geek to another) have gone back and forth about the *real* meaning of that scene. My two cents? It simply means, choose your own adventure. Decide what happens next, and never forget that healthy curiosity is the best gift, leading to more questions, experiences, and moments. School is kinda like *The Matrix*: a strange universe where the truth is elusive and everybody fronts like they have all the answers. (Trust me, they don't.) And each action can pull you toward your destiny or push you away from it. Sometimes you'll follow the herd because there's safety in numbers and blending in, and sometimes you'll get a little circus with it, because you're sick of the crowd and your shade of awesome is too neon bright for the crew.

When I say circus, I'm not advising you to contort your double-jointed body into an Auntie Anne's pretzel or swallow fire, just don't be afraid to be an individual, or to swallow the red pill when all of your friends are reaching for the blue one. Different is dope, or as Angelina Jolie says, "Different is good."

I don't know Angelina personally, but we're both a little bit circus and share the same view on this topic. She gave one of the best acceptance speeches in 2015 and it wasn't to a room of designer gowns and tailored tuxedos at the Oscars. At the Nickelodeon Kids' Choice Awards, Angelina snagged the trophy for Best Villain for her role in *Maleficent* and she told the screaming crowd: "When I was little, like Maleficent, I was told that I was different. And I felt out of place—too loud, too full of fire, never good at sitting still, never good at fitting in. And then one day I realized something, something that I hope you all realize: Different is good. And as your villain, I would also say, cause a little trouble—it's good for you."

You Had The Power All Along, My Dear

Like Neo, you were given the power to make decisions. All of these options make it confusing and terrifying too. But it comes down to this: You're either the star of your show, or the supporting actress in someone's blockbuster. Gayle Forman, author of the touching young adult novel, *If I Stay*, put it this way in that book: "Sometimes you make choices in life and sometimes choices make you." Okay, Gayle, get outta my head! I'm so with you on this one. (Side note: If you haven't read the book, which I definitely recommend, then check out the movie starring the wonderful Chloë Grace Moretz.)

I totally believe we're the sum of every choice (hey, Gayle, hey!) that we've ever made. For example, I decided to talk long before I learned how to walk. Ma insists that I had full conversations while holding court on the couch as my playmates did the toddler wobble on the floor. It makes perfect sense to me: Deep down, something inside of me knew I needed to be heard. There were also times when I really needed to speak up, but couldn't find the words.

When we lived in a four-story walk-up, Ma only let me play with a few of the neighbors' kids. She just preferred to keep a safe distance until we got to know people better. So when a new family moved next door to us with a boy who was a year or two older than I was, I was happy to make a new friend—or so I thought. I spent most of my time hanging out with my brother and male cousins, so chilling with a boy wasn't foreign to me. That is, until The Neighbor's Kid decided that I was his personal shish kebab. Maybe I'd seen one too many afterschool specials about kids burning their homes to the ground and I knew this situation wouldn't end well—for me. He grabbed a book of matches and started lighting small pieces of paper on fire, then quickly stomping them out. My stomach got queasy, and my gut told my head that I was in trouble, but I was too scared to open my mouth. I hadn't learned to rely on it—yet. The next thing you know, The Neighbor's Kid singed the lower left side of my face, just below my lip. It left a small scar that has faded over time, but I couldn't explain to my mother why I let this boy near me with matches, much less my face. (I was too excited when they moved out of the building.) It was a lesson: Trust your gut. It started working for me at an early age and the more I relied on it, the more it's helped me choose my own adventures, and helped me speak up. It's never steered me wrong. So what you should do when it's your turn to take the wheel? You know I have a few ideas.

★★ *Star Tips* ★★

1. **Begin with the end in mind:** The author of this statement is freakin' brilliant. Folks attribute it to Sean Covey, who wrote *7 Habits of Highly Effective Teens*, but I swear one of my elementary school English teachers drilled this screw into my peanut head a long time ago. This gem invites you to ask

yourself: What do I want to happen? Which outcome will make me do cart-wheels down the hallway? A clear idea will help you choose the right path.

2. **Think about it:** No one should ever make a decision without thinking it over, or worse, believing that it'll work itself out. What's that about? I cringe when characters say that on TV because it's a recipe for disaster. Why not give the situation—like whether to stay at a huge, overpopulated school with lame electives another year or transfer to a smaller school with the HTML coding elective—the attention it deserves? Going into something blind or being passive will lead to "I didn't know" when the funky stuff hits the fan. Even if you're pressed to give an answer or submit an application in three days, don't be impulsive. Consider your options before taking the leap.

3. **Collect info and write it down:** Gather valuable intel from reliable sources. Notice the *reliable* part. When it comes to transferring to a new school, your homies aren't the go-to source for this. Their opinions are bi-ased. You'll be accused of breaking up the crew and run the risk of being swayed by all that "we'll miss you" talk. Yeah, yeah, yeah, go that way with all of that. That's not a good enough reason to stay in a situation that sucks. Consult your advisor, one of the Fave Five, a former classmate at the new school, and—*gasp!*—your parents. The advisor may ride hard for your cur-rent school in public, but in private she could confess that a smaller learning environment is better for your needs. Write the challenge across the top of a piece of paper and put the desired outcome at the bottom. Make bullet points for pros and cons or different scenarios. Draw arrows from the bullet points that lead to your desired outcome. Jot down the consequences, so you can see how one decision may positively or negatively influence every-thing else.

4. **Do a gut check:** After years of becoming an expert on choosing my own adventure, I've learned to trust my instincts. My gut has become more in tune with my concerns, values, and goals after years of experience. That flip-flop moment in my stomach, that "I'm about to throw up a burger and fries" feeling is a signal that danger is speeding toward me with a set of faulty brakes. Often, when I've ignored it, I've ended up in funky situations, like the time my motorcycle-driving date tried to force me to have sex with him.

My gut warned me that going to his house was a no-no, but I ignored it and went anyway. It didn't take long before dude attempted to pin me down and rip off my clothes. I fought him off, kicked him in the balls, and ended up unharmed. I was pretty shaken up, but lucky; it could've been much worse.

5. **Ask yourself, *What will happen if I...*:** If your gut isn't a trusted resource yet, then it's time to map out the possibilities and the consequences of your actions, especially for monster decision making, i.e. *What'll happen if I have unprotected sex?* As you know from sex ed class and episodes of *Teen Mom* and Internet images of herpes, there are a few different ways things can go left, as in an unplanned pregnancy, an STD (including HIV/AIDs), and all hell breaking loose when your parents find out. Having sex is already major, but trusting another person with your health? No bueno. Don't ever do that.

6. **Create an action plan:** What good is all of this examination, data collection, and insight if you don't do something with it? It's go time. Your decision to attend a summer camp for teen writers in another state could just be a footnote in your life story, or the moment that influences everything moving forward. The Social Security Administration (SSA) hired me a few weeks after college graduation and I was making good money (yay for moolah, baby!), but I was bored and the job had nothing to do with my major. In my mind, this was just a temporary situation and all part of the master plan until I landed a media gig. I was thankful to have employment, which paid for expensive club hopping in NYC, dinners with friends, weekend road trips, and the small amount of rent Ma charged. Three months into my stint at the SSA, my friend (and sorority sister) Melissa Washington-Harris, who I'd met during my internship at *ESSENCE*, asked if I wanted to interview for her job. You know my answer was "yes." That internship wasn't just a wonderful memory, it was a turning point. If I hadn't met Melissa, who knows how long it would've taken me to get something in the publishing game.

7. **Understand decision vs. outcome:** Making smart, informed decisions takes practice, especially when there's more than one option involved, i.e. you get three promposals or offers to sing at three anniversary parties on the same day. Just know that while you have the power to control the decision, you don't control the outcome. What does this mean? Let me put it

this way: If you choose the cutest boy of the three to be your date, he could turn out to be as exciting as popping a pimple. If you sing at an anniversary party with the hefty payday—instead of warbling for free at your cousin's shindig—the sound system could die in the middle of your rendition of Justin Timberlake's "Mirrors." That would suck, not just because I love me some JT, but because a romantic moment crashed and burned. I'm just sayin'.

8. **Rewind the tape:** You know how athletes watch replays of their games? This is the same concept. After you've made a big decision and settled into something new, take a moment to reflect on what worked and what didn't, but first congratulate yourself for confronting that Big Decision with solid thinking and avoiding that wack it-will-work-itself-out route.

Yo, What's The Scenario?

It's time to take your skills on a test drive. Read the scenarios below and, given what you know about making decisions—and trusting your gut—note how you'd handle the following situations.

Scenario No. 1

Everyone (including your besties) thinks the New Girl is a lil' weird, but you don't. You've spoken to her and you guys share similar interests, including a love for henna designs. She invites you to hang out at her house to learn some DIY henna tricks on Friday. You happily accept. Days later, Popular Girl says you and your friends should swing by her all-girls kickback, which is also on Friday. Your girls can't wait to be in the mix, but you aren't feeling this at all. She's been icy toward you for the last two months—now suddenly Popular Girl wants to thaw the cold war. Your gut says this is a setup, but you don't have any proof. **What do you do?**

_____

_____

_____

_____

Scenario No. 2

Cute Boy with the Annoying Girlfriend starts showing you attention on the low. At first, the compliments are flattering, especially because you were feeling down. Then he whispers inappropriate comments in your ear in the gym. You threaten to tell his girl, but he doesn't stop. It makes things worse and Cute Boy sends Snapchat photos of his naked body parts. Okay, now you're steaming. Rumors fly fast and furious and his girl accuses you of trying to break them up. Your sister suggests taking a screenshot of his inappropriate pictures and putting him on blast. Your brother offers to break his texting finger, both arms, and nose. **What do you do?**

_____

_____

_____

_____

_____

_____

_____

_____

_____

_____

_____

_____

_____

_____

_____

Scenario No. 3

Globetrotting Auntie uses her connects to get you a three-week internship with a tech company in Japan. She'll finance everything, including plane tickets, meals, and spending money. You're eager to put another stamp in your passport, but the dates overlap with basketball camp, which will boost your chances of making the varsity team next year. Auntie drops a few yen in your lap and says this is a no-brainer. Mom and Dad say the decision is yours to make. **What do you do?**

_____

_____

_____

_____

_____

_____

_____

_____

_____

_____

_____

_____

_____

_____

Scenario No. 4

Your school's talent show MC loses her voice (she strained it pretending to be Natalie La Rose during karaoke) and offers your name as her replacement. Before you accept, decline, or run for the exit, the MC hands over the script and rehearsal notes for tomorrow's big event. The production manager is freaking out and gives you a super short amount of time to think it over. The next fifteen minutes are crucial. One of your classmates says it's a perfect way to showcase your comedic talent between breaks. **What do you do?**

_____

_____

_____

_____

_____

_____

_____

_____

_____

_____

_____

_____

_____

_____

_____

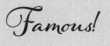

CHEAT SHEET NO. 7

Three things on my adventure list are:

_____

_____

_____

_____

_____

My desired outcomes for all three adventures are:

_____

_____

_____

_____

_____

I can trust my gut because:

_____

_____

_____

_____

_____

8

FAILURE IS THE REAL F-BOMB (YES, IT'S AN OPTION)

"There is freedom waiting for you, on the breezes of the sky, And you ask, 'What if I fall?' Oh, but my darling, What if you fly?"

—ERIN HANSON

We're all scared to fail. Screwing up on the chemistry test. Choking in the first round of the national spelling bee. Doing a belly flop into the pool at a swim meet. Goofs—puny or gargantuan, public or private—are inevitable. I'm sharing this with you because nobody schooled me, and I want you to know how to handle yourself.

You and I are in good company. The most successful people admit to learning the most from their failures, and those boo-boos helped them succeed. As much as we fear it, in a very strange way, we need it too. I know you're reading this like, *What is she talking about?* Think about it like this: If you win the junior class president spot by a landslide (or even by five measly votes!), that success gives you the confidence to lead your classmates and maybe run for the senior class spot next year. But if you lose the election, that failure is feedback that you probably don't want to hear about preparation, campaign messaging, and timing. It's a chance to celebrate what you did right but also examine what went wrong. Few of us enjoy the post-game review, so we handle a crushing defeat in two ways:

1. We dive under the covers with a pint of Häagen-Dazs and refuse to emerge until every spoonful of cookies and cream is gone (and our pride is frozen/numb to any snarky "I told you so" comments) and decide against any activity that requires taking a risk. EVER.
2. We suck up the loss. Acknowledge that it stings, get feedback from the Fave Five, and use it as motivation to come back harder or take a similar chance in another arena. (Maybe the vocabulary bee is a better look? Because you flubbed spelling e-x-t-e-m-p-o-r-a-n-e-o-u-s.)

Before I became lactose intolerant, I was guilty of running through door number one more times than I'd like to admit, especially as my dad owned a Baskin-Robbins.

My story: In the eighth grade I'd said I was "done" with IS68 and ready to graduate, even though my school went up to the ninth grade. I don't know which cuckoo bird made that an option for us back then, but I took the baton and ran with it because my friends were graduating and I couldn't be the child left behind. No, ma'am. I was outta there with roller skates on and so very clueless about high school.

Ma said I wasn't ready. Looking back, I see why: I was thirteen, short, skinny, and couldn't bust a grape in a fruit fight. She envisioned the worst, i.e. boys trying to get into my pretty panties (well, she was right there); mean girls using my eyes as punching bags and stuffing me into a locker; me morphing into a socially awkward kid intimidated by older teens. I disagreed—loudly—in the street with a temper tantrum worthy of an Emmy nomination for Outstanding Lead Actress in a Miniseries or Movie. Surprisingly, Ma caved and signed the form releasing me from middle school.

On my first day at Graphic Communication Arts (GCA), I realized why Ma was so concerned. We didn't have lockers, but I did witness a new kid getting dumped into a garbage can on Freshmen Friday. This was hardly the carefree back-to-school situation seen today in those cute J.C. Penney commercials. One of the many benefits of being a shy girl was that I spent my time observing crazy from a distance. I became an expert in dos and don'ts, rituals, cliques, habits of my classmates, and how fast I could run from the lunchroom to the nearest exit if someone decided it was my turn to land in a pile of lunch meat facedown. I flew under the tripwire while studying my place in the food chain. I wouldn't let Ma have the satisfaction of being right about high school.

Like every high school, GCA had its cliques: club kids, jocks, gangs, nerds, bohemians, weed heads, etc. It was easy to find your tribe. Heads rarely escaped their groups intact. You could be kicked out, but chucking up the deuces to the club kids to vibe with the nerds was unicorn rare. At some point I figured out that high school was about fitting into boxes, so I passed on all of them. I'd done that in elementary and reinvented myself at IS68. This girl refused to go back. While it was terrifying to run solo, I found the courage to rock with whom I wanted to. I rode the train home with the bohemians and ate lunch with the journalism kids. I danced with my bestie in the talent show before a fight broke out and messed up the night. I had a boyfriend (or two) in a gang. (That's not a recommendation to follow my lead, these are just #facts.)

Somehow, I became popular. But not in the way you see in teen movies with the queen bee rocking the latest clothes and bags. My classmates knew me as the girl from Black History Club, the talent show, or advisory council, or because of my "Think Smart" column in the student newspaper.

All of this newfound attention made me think I had to be perfect. There were invisible limits that I'd set up for myself, with no room to experiment. I worried about what everyone would think—when they probably weren't thinking about me at all! Like a hamster on a wheel, I ran around in a circle going nowhere fast until I decided to hop off and stop caring about all those imaginary eyes secretly judging my moves. I asked myself (and you will too), *Are you willing to miss out on opportunities just because you might fail?*

Nah, I wasn't ready to do that. The geek/leader in me dreamed about being senior class president, which meant organizing the prom and senior trip and being the mouthpiece for the class. I'd never done of any of this before. Our advisor had the worst rep; his favorite word was "no" and he often told students to "play in traffic." My classmates avoided him because his rants were legendary. Clearly, I'd taken a few loony pills because I convinced myself that I could make our advisor listen to my ideas. This bold move had all of the ingredients of an epic fail.

The process was simple: The candidates campaigned and delivered speeches and the senior class voted (with a show of hands) while we stared at the sea of smiling/smirking faces in the auditorium. All kinds of negative thoughts raced through my head: What if none of my classmates clapped or voted for me? I considered backing out several times, including minutes before I stood at the podium in the auditorium. I felt like throwing up as the students voted for each candidate. Everything moved in slow motion and the sound seemed distorted as the advisor announced that I won. I played it cool, but inside my heart my pounded so hard I thought I'd burst right down the middle. I was ecstatic and terrified at the same time. It's one of my top twenty favorite moments of my young life, but it didn't prepare me for when I'd fall flat on my face. The only thing that prepared me for that was falling flat on my face. Every politician, athlete, singer, athlete, or actor will tell you about the rush associated with winning. It's indescribable, but nothing compares to the courage you get from taking a risk and winning—despite the possibility of crashing and burning. Every time you succeed, it motivates you to tackle a new challenge, something more difficult. Failure can stop you in your tracks—or it can help you build a thick skin to survive in the world.

Side note: My advisor's bark was worse than his bite. He ended up being super cool and never yelled at me. He did try to kiss Ma in the mouth at graduation, but I'll end that story right here.

That Time I Screwed Up At Work

Writers are required to have alligator skin to survive. We're constantly pitching ideas and rejection is part of the game. Editors will say this concept is brilliant or that idea sucks. We don't take it personally and we keep swinging until we hit a home run. I'd pitched a cover story for *Juicy* magazine about a singer who was making a serious career comeback. Her new music was poppin' and she was killing it on a popular television show. And Miss R&B Chick wasn't so untouchable that her publicist would ignore my email, as I'd interviewed the vocalist before. The odds were in my favor.

Before I finish the rest of this story, please understand the importance of a cover story in print. Cover stories are gold. The goal is get all the precious metal that *isn't* buzzed about on every corner of the Internet. It isn't an easy

Famous!

task when everyone loves freebies via blogs and social media.

My interview date was set (kinda) with Miss R&B Chick's publicist. I flew from New York City to Los Angeles and stayed at the Andaz West Hollywood. When I arrived, the game plan changed more than once. It went from meeting on the set of her video shoot to her dressing room to her favorite restaurant. I wasn't a newbie to the celebrity chase (read: runaround) and last-minute switch mode. I offered my suite as a possible location—anything to make life easier for the artist. Her publicist strung me along for two days until he finally admitted that Miss R&B Chick wasn't available for the interview. I scrambled to fix this disaster, but I had nada.

I couldn't blame the artist because I wasn't sure she even knew I was in L.A. for the interview. But I was pissed that the publicist—who'd started sending my calls to voicemail—overpromised and under delivered. As I called my editor to explain that my cover subject was missing in action, I calculated how much company money I'd spent—plane ticket, hotel, rental car, gas, and meals—to return with a pile of receipts, minus a great interview. The news made its way to *Juicy*'s publisher. Was I embarrassed? Yup. Times two. It was a gut punch. My plan failed. It forced me to look at where I went wrong and be more cautious with publicists who promise the moon but can't deliver any celestial bodies. That was an expensive lesson to learn—but it didn't stop me from pitching ideas.

Years later, I read a Pinterest quote that reminded me of that situation and other slip ups. It said, "Mistakes are proof that we're trying." Don't be afraid or paralyzed by your missteps, Star. Life is trial and error.

★★★ *Star Tips* ★★★

1. **Regret, not:** Okay, so your comedy routine bombed at the local talent show. Ouch. I won't say don't freak out. You're going to spaz. That's human nature. So go ahead and scream into a pillow. Grab your boxing gloves and hit the heavy bag at the gym. Go for a run in the park. Have your moment where you get it all out. Then congratulate yourself. You put yourself out there; don't regret taking the chance. All of your comedic godmothers were booed or dodged chicken bones that were tossed onstage during their act.

Jokes have to be written and tested and rewritten or deleted. Keep bringing the funny.

2. **School yourself:** Class is in session and this time you're the teacher *and* the student. Learn to critique, not criticize your mistakes. There's a difference. A critique looks for awesome, by honestly reviewing what works and what doesn't. It requires the kindness and compassion that you'd give to strangers. You aren't allowed to put yourself down! Grab a pen and pad and answer the following questions: What did I do well? How can I improve? Was I prepared? What interfered? Did my nerves get the best of me? What do I need to do next time? What did I learn about myself? Answering these questions will push you to be better the next time you step into the spotlight.

3. **Don't stop trying:** This makes me think of Vera Wang. She's a famous designer known for gorgeous wedding gowns, engagement rings, cosmetics, and more, but in her youth she aspired to be a professional figure skater. Well, a funny thing happened when Vera didn't make the Olympic team. After college she was hired as a temporary assistant at *Vogue* and worked her way up to become one of the magazine's youngest fashion editors. She stayed there for fifteen years before joining Ralph Lauren as a design director and eventually becoming an entrepreneur. Vera never stopped loving skating and even designed outfits for athletes in the sport. I'm sure failing to qualify for the Olympic team was devastating at the time, but it seems like Vera ended up exactly where she needed to be. Always stay hungry for more, and be open to opportunities that may lead you down a new path.

4. **Hit up someone on your team:** Remember your Fave Five? Well, they're in it to support you during the rollercoaster ride. Call one of them and recap what happened. Don't leave out the horrible parts. Getting the story out of your system to a sympathetic ear is helpful. She probably has stories about losing an important client, fumbling a moneymaking idea, or accusing the wrong person of theft. Listen to how she recovered from an embarrassing blunder.

5. **Shake it off:** It's time to do something you enjoy and change the color on your mood ring. Pick your favorite activity, call a friend, and have at it. It can

be as simple as treating yourself to frozen yogurt, running in the park with your dog, abusing a ball in a faux ping pong tournament, or reenacting a video with your friends. (C'mon, dancing around the house and singing into your brush never gets old.) Do something to move your confidence meter back to where it should be, because that flub was a minor setback.

Brag Much?

Everyone should create a Bragging Rights list with at least ten victories. It helps to remember your accomplishments, especially after bombing at the teen comedy club. We can rattle off each and every time we messed up, but quickly forget about all the times we rocked. I know bragging gets a bad rap because it's seen as being cocky, but this isn't about being self-centered and telling everyone how dope you are. (Yes, that's annoying.) This list boosts your confidence after a trip and fall. Don't be ashamed to celebrate yourself. Stick it on your mirror or keep it in your dresser and pull it out as needed.

Turn to the next page to get started.

Bragging Rights

1. _____

2. _____

3. _____

4. _____

5. _____

6. _____

7. _____

8. _____

9. _____

10. _____

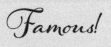

CHEAT SHEET NO. 8

Usually when my idea fails I:

_____

_____

_____

Now I know that I have to:

_____

_____

_____

_____

_____

Next time I won't be afraid to:

_____

_____

_____

_____

_____

_____

_____

9

THE LIES TASTE AWFUL, BUT THE TRUTH IS DELICIOUS

"I hope you know that this will go down on your permanent record."

—VIOLENT FEMMES, "KISS OFF"

There are a few lies you've already heard in school and, cough, at home, like *we're almost there* during a painfully long road trip; Santa Claus put the wrong address in the GPS; it tastes just like chicken; the Tooth Fairy was hit with budget cuts, and, my least favorite, "We'll see." Whenever Ma or my teacher said this they were attempting to let me down easy, but it would've saved me valuable nagging time if they'd told me "no" upfront. By the way, frog legs *do* taste like chicken (they're really good with hot sauce) and your parents worked hard to buy all that expensive crap for Christmas when you were 10 years old, so thank them for buying stuff that doesn't even matter to you anymore. Here are a few more falsehoods you'll hear and some truths to go along with them.

Lie No. 1: *These test results will go on your permanent record and follow you—forever.*

Truth No. 1: I've never seen the contents of my permanent record (PR). Never. And no one has offered me a peek at it either, but growing up it tormented me. Now that I mention it, I'm insanely curious about this document that teachers waved over my head to keep me in line. Well, maybe not me, but definitely my peers. I mean, for the most part, I didn't color too far outside the lines, but teachers were always warning us that our actions would be summarized, alphabetized, and stored in some ugly file cabinet that housed the dreaded PR. You know what that thing is, right? It's a snapshot of your life: Grades, city and statewide exam scores, placement test results, attendance records, honors, athletic participation, health info, and disciplinary actions, of course. So if you got busted bullying a classmate on Instagram, there's probably a note covering the five Ws (who, what, when, where, why) of your actions in your PR. Or, if you were absent more than one hundred days (of the one hundred and eighty day school year) like a student was on Sundance Channel's *Dream School*, that's definitely in there too.

I was a good student and aced many of my classes (with the exception of math, but you already knew that) and every year during the statewide or Regents exams I'd get nervous, lose focus, and forget math formulas and earth-science facts. Knowing that these scores would be inked in my PR made everything in the official test booklet smash together like one gigantic run-on sentence. It made me worry about my future college or employer flipping past my attendance record to read my lackluster math score—because when my teacher said this stupid folder would follow me forever, she meant until I died, right? I thought colleges and my first employer would get access to it and my application because I'd barely passed The Big Test. Clearly, my brain was working overtime and none of this happened. We're so much more than good grades or so-so test scores and the contents of our PR, which doesn't tell the full picture. The girl sitting next to you might be horrible at math, but she knows how to read and write music. That makes her special.

When I applied for college, no one asked for a copy of my permanent record. Admissions counselors wanted my SAT scores, transcript, personal essay, and a list of extracurricular activities. When the ghost of the PR no longer haunted me, I realized it was a way to encourage us to behave, care about the choices we make, and take the exams seriously. I took it too far and made myself macadamia nuts. The PR didn't hold me back or push me forward, and there was so much more to my story than student-of-the-week accolades.

If you attend a private school or are able to opt out of major exams, this is all foreign to you. And if you are intimidated by the SAT, just know that some colleges, like Amberton University in Texas and American University in D.C., deemphasize this exam in their entrance process. Then there are others who skip the SAT altogether, like the Fashion Institute of Technology (FIT) in New York City and Goddard College in Vermont. For all my college-bound Stars who are completely over taking tests, this is an awesome research project.

Lie No. 2: *This isn't a competition.*
Truth No. 2: Um, excuse me, but everything in life says otherwise. Believe that. Stats, bar graphs, tests, elections, and lists highlighting who made the most money selling The Amazing Widget dominate our culture. Think about your school: If this isn't a competition, why does the student with the highest GPA represent the class at graduation? Why does the student government association hold elections and tabulate votes? Why does the scorekeeper track home runs? The answer is simple: It's a competition. Some people are wired to race toward whatever finish line is placed up ahead. Others wander off track permanently, or until they discover where they excel. Still, every contest, race, and competition isn't worth your time. Decide where you need to be. Explore. Try something new. Leave your comfort zone. Stop thinking the answer is at school. Find your gift, or be open to it finding you.

In business circles, the name Sophia Amoruso is a big deal. Prior to 2006, she was just a young woman working minimum wage jobs who loved vintage clothing. But Sophia was floating from one day to the next. She even admits to dumpster diving, i.e. finding her meals in the trash. In her book #GIRLBOSS, she says don't knock a throwaway bagel until you've tried it. Now I'm not a squeamish germaphobe and I've been guilty of calling the two-second rule if a meatball hits the floor, but I'll pass on an everything bagel smeared with garbage pal goodies. But I digress.

I became slightly (okay, very) obsessed with Sophia's intriguing story. The San Diego, California, native went from being "directionless" to finding her purpose (or, the place she should compete) after landing a gig checking IDs at an art school. Mind you, Sophia took this job only because she needed health insurance for a hernia. Still, on her downtime she opened an eBay store called Nasty Gal Vintage. Seven years later, she became the founder and CEO of a hundred-million dollar online business (now called Nasty Gal) with three hundred and fifty employees.

Her career jumpstarted later than her parents would've liked, but once Sophia discovered her star power she remained focused on kicking major booty in the online market. In 2015, she stepped down from the CEO spot to play to her strengths yet again, to oversee the creative and marketing arms of Nasty Gal. It didn't make sense for Sophia to compete in the fast food industry, but she needed that job at Subway and then the gig at the art school to put her on the path to finding the race that mattered most in *her* life. Sometimes your fiercest competitor is starring you in the mirror, watching you brush your teeth every morning.

Lie No. 3: *Express yourself. Speak up. We're listening.*
Truth No. 3: I found this hard to believe in high school when GCA's administration requested that Mr. Young (no relation to me) remove the poster of Malcolm X from our black history classroom. The class was an elective, but it was super important to me, especially since my previous encounters with my history were short entries on the African-American holocaust and Dr. Martin Luther King, Jr. Ma and my grandmother were history buffs, so I knew that my teachers skipped heroes like Sojourner Truth and stories about how enslaved blacks fought alongside the British army during the Revolutionary War in exchange for their freedom.

The assistant vice principal was reluctant to discuss the situation. In my mind, if my school was called Graphic Communication Arts, then we needed to communicate. We had a meeting where he claimed that images of Malcolm X would encourage the students to be violent. What? He couldn't be serious. Clearly he'd never stopped by the cafeteria to witness Freshmen Friday shenanigans and was oblivious to the Decepticons roaming the hallways. The poster hanging in our classroom didn't influence their behavior. The AP didn't know or didn't care to know how Malcolm X's message evolved after being ousted from the Nation of Islam and his trip to Mecca. He no longer hated white people and regretted many of his previous comments.

The conversation ended with an ultimatum: Remove the poster or Mr. Young would lose his job as the social studies and black history teacher. While I wanted to keep the image, it wasn't worth my favorite instructor hitting the unemployment line. The poster came down. I never shook the feeling that the AP heard me, but wasn't really *listening*. If you attend one of those schools where the students really do have a say, please know that I'm completely and insanely jealous. Also, use that power. Seriously. Continue (or start) to use your voice in your school and community. It's a fabulous training ground for stepping up to the mic and becoming an activist.

Lie No. 4: *It doesn't matter what you look like on the outside.*
Truth No. 4: It shouldn't matter what you look on the outside, but as soon as you leave your house you realize very few people are checking for your *insides*. Don't forget about our friend Lizzie Velasquez. Now, I believe that the invisible cocktail of generosity, kindness, and benevolence swirling around inside of us is more important than having a cute as a button nose and beautifully sculpted eyebrows. I've seen an attribute like selflessness turn an average-looking woman into a beauty once you see her become a foster parent to four children or feed homeless families year round. I don't know what you've heard but big hearts are all kinds of sexy. (On the flip side, I've also seen some folks whose insides are so rotten...well, let's just leave that one there.)

I know that some of your friends haven't reached the don't-judge-a-book-by-its-cover status. I'm not criticizing them (or you). It took me a minute to get there too. I've spent some time forming opinions about boys and girls based on their looks—even with my crooked teeth, lopsided boobs, and bowlegs! Chipmunk cheeks, saucer-shaped eyes, or copper-colored skin can make you the recipient of some unfriendly comments. Should we celebrate diverse facial features? Sure. Do we? Nope. We attack them. Laugh. Call them ugly. You know how cruel your peers can be.

But think about this: the facial feature that people mock can become the very same feature that people covet, or attempt to copy as an adult. I knew girls who cried because their full, juicy lips were called "soup coolers." Fast forward to the current day and lip augmentation is all the rage. Suddenly women want lips like Angelina Jolie, Scarlett Johansson, Jessica Alba, or Kylie Jenner.

I've learned everything I know about embracing my beauty (and the gorgeousness of others) from a Khalil Gibran quote. The writer/poet said, "Beauty is not in the face, beauty is a light in the heart." This statement has helped me ignore other people's negative comments about my eyes, nose, lips, and body. Remember this: you are more than just a collection of parts for people to adore or criticize; your actions transform you into a whole person; and the light in your heart determines what you *really* look like to the outside world.

Lie No. 5: *These are the best years of your life.*
Truth No. 5: Whoever said this hasn't done anything cool as an adult—ever. Maybe this person was the captain of the softball team or voted most athletic and that's the best part of her highlight reel. Welp, that sucks for them. College was waaaaay better than high school, and getting the keys to my first apartment felt great until it was time to pay the rent.

Don't get me wrong. High school was dope, but if I recall correctly, and I know that I do, I shared a room with my baby sister, had limited funds, and no male company was allowed in the house without supervision. That's not best-moment material in my book. Nor is the time Ma dragged me out of a house party in our building and the DJ called her the "curfew police."

I agree with Mindy Kaling that no one cares that you were best whatever in high school. It's immediately insignificant the day after graduation. In her hilarious book, *Is Everyone Hanging Out Without Me? (And Other Concerns)* she said: "What I've noticed is that almost no one who was a big star in high school is also big star later in life. For us overlooked kids, it's so wonderfully *fair*." Translation? The best actress at your school probably won't take home a Golden Globe trophy. But the girl who ate her hair for lunch and knew all the answers in physics could be a contender. Believe that. Mindy wasn't one of the cool kids and she didn't have a boyfriend in high school, but a few years later (at age twenty-four) she was the first female writer for the hit TV show *The Office*. I'd say her current situation is way better than it was at her alma mater, Buckingham Browne & Nichols.

If the "best days of your life" concept is still troubling to you, just know this: Hair-Eating Girl at your school will probably find her tribe, reinvent herself, or take an acting class just for fun. She'll discover that's she crazy good at morphing into characters and maybe even writing must-see thrillers. After a while, her credits will go from the flier of a local play to the screen of this summer's highly anticipated blockbuster movie, followed by that Golden Globe nomination I mentioned earlier.

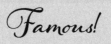

CHEAT SHEET NO. 9

The biggest, most awful lie I've been told was:

_____

_____

_____

_____

But the delicious truth is:

_____

_____

_____

_____

I've decided to express myself by:

_____

_____

_____

_____

_____

_____

_____

Star Crush: **Malala Yousafzai**

One of the most famous teenagers in the world doesn't sing pop songs or dance in her undies to get your attention. Malala Yousafzai simply wants girls in her hometown of Swat Valley in Pakistan—and around the world—to attend school without fear of being killed. The Taliban (an Islamic fundamentalist political order) in Pakistan and Afghanistan ordered girls' schools be shut down because, to this group, it isn't necessary to educate girls. They've already tried to silence Malala and have successfully murdered many others.

Bombing schools and killing innocent people was scary to Malala, who dreamed of becoming a doctor, and to her father, Ziauddin Yousafzai, an activist who'd opened a school for girls many years before. Malala loathed the Taliban and at 11 years old, she bravely voiced her opinion, alongside her dad, in *The New York Times* documentary *Class Dismissed: Malala's Story* by Adam B. Ellick. She also wrote about her worries and how dangerous the Taliban could be (under the pen name Gul Makai) for a now-famous BBC blog.

On October 9, 2012, a Taliban gunman jumped on a school bus and demanded to know: "Who is Malala?" He fired three shots at point-blank range, hitting his target and injuring two other girls. One of the bullets hit the left side of Malala's forehead and traveled into her face and shoulder. Although she was rushed to a local clinic, a military hospital, and then finally to England for additional treatment, no one expected her to survive. Thankfully, surgeons were able to reconstruct her skull and repair her face. Today, she's only slightly disfigured from that near-fatal attack and Malala continues to fight for girls' education. She told Diane Sawyer in an *ABC News* interview: "I think death didn't want to kill me." Malala also recounted that incident on the bus in a book aptly titled: *I Am Malala: The Girl Who Stood Up for Education and Was Shot by the Taliban.*

One year after being shot, Malala won Pakistan's National Youth Peace Prize, and it was later renamed the National Malala Peace Prize in her honor. On Malala's sixteenth birthday on July 12, 2013, she spoke at the United Nations Youth Assembly and they dubbed it Malala Day. But the very humble speaker shifted the focus to the world stage. She said, "Malala Day is not my day. Today is the day of every woman, every boy and every girl who have raised their voice for their rights... Thousands of people have been killed by the terrorists and millions have been injured. I'm just *one* of them. So here I stand...one girl among many. I speak, not for myself, but for those without voice to be heard."

Months after Malala's unforgettable UN speech, she was nominated for a Nobel Peace Prize, and won the esteemed award in October 2014. She shares the distinction with Indian activist Kailash Satyarthi, who advocates for children's rights and rallies against child labor. At age 17, Malala became the youngest Nobel laureate in history.

10

YOU WANT MORE? COOL.
GO GET IT.

"If you obey all the rules, you miss all the fun."

—KATHARINE HEPBURN

In 2005, Steve Jobs offered a brilliant parting statement to the graduating class of Stanford University. It was this: "Stay hungry. Stay foolish." If I could tat these words somewhere on my body I would, but I fear pain and permanent ink. It's one of the best graduation speeches, no—make that speeches, period—I've ever heard, and I spend a lot of time watching Ted Talks online. That's complete geek mode. I know. I'm not the least bit ashamed. Put it on your watch list. I live for people's personal history and in this speech, Steve told three important life stories that eventually influenced his development work on tech must-haves, like iTunes, the iPhone, and the iPad.

Steve admitted to finding an image of a long, winding road that seemed to lead to the sky with the caption: "Stay hungry. Stay foolish." It was on the back of the last issue of the *Whole Earth Catalog*. It resonated with him because his life was full of setbacks, starting at birth. The couple who were on board to adopt him decided at the last minute that they wanted a girl. So he ended up with another family who didn't finish college, but they'd promised Steve's biological mother that he'd attend. Steve did go to college for a while, but dropped out.

I didn't know any of this. I assumed he was born into a semi-perfect existence and his parents nurtured his love for all things tech. His speech became even more intriguing to me because life is messy and the solutions to our challenges aren't the happy endings we see in movies. Like me, Steve believed that all the dots from your past connect in your future. Allow me to give you my interpretation of those two powerful lines.

Stay hungry: Everybody knows to fuel the body, but feeding the brain is top priority too. I'm not talking about the fundamentals and fancy algorithms you learn in school. Some of that you use daily, i.e. reading the menu at your favorite burger joint or calculating the thirty percent discount on a T-shirt. I'm referring to the discoveries waiting to be explored *outside* of the place you're legally mandated to be for almost two hundred days of the year.

I've taken HTML coding classes, read some of those books in the *Dummies* series, and even sent a handwritten note to a total stranger, asking her to meet me for coffee. Why? I'd read about a chichi corporate dinner party she'd organized, and I craved (get it?) intel about this fascinating special events job. This woman graciously talked to me for twenty minutes in Starbucks. In exchange for her time, I treated her to some venti mocha fabulousness. I was prepared with some key questions, listened, and took notes. It was a gratifying moment—never underestimate the power of a dope conversation.

That experience (and others) reminds me to pay it forward, and I do when young women email me or hit me up on social media. I'm not pushing you to request meetings with total strangers—but think about the adults in your friendship tree. Maybe your mother hired an event planner for her business and there's an opportunity to connect with that person via Skype or ooVoo. Or maybe you can shadow your mom's client in her office. I believe in the six degrees of separation concept and use it to connect with people who can help me untangle messy situations or just offer been-there-done-that advice. This can work for you too, when you spot an opportunity and spring into action.

Stay foolish: This is my favorite part of the quote. Remember when everybody was running around screaming, "YOLO" ("You only live once")? Yeah, blame Drake for that one. Some thought that was the universal green light to catch a case and act the fool. They missed the real point. YOLO and stay foolish are actually cousins. Both are about trying something new. Think about entrepreneurs, inventors, and creatives who are bold enough to whip up something that didn't exist before. It's tricky. It's risky. Will people love it or hate it?

Take the founders of Instagram. Kevin Systrom and Mike Krieger loved playing around with cameras as kids and were into the old cameras that billed themselves as "instant." At first, these guys thought taking cool pictures meant having access to a professional camera and a few snazzy art school credits. But as camera phones improved, that belief didn't hold true. So they used their interests to create Instagram. Adding filters was key to enhancing a basic image and transforming it into something special, and later they added a video option to their super-popular app. More than three hundred million people use IG—and all because these guys loved instant photos. C'mon, admit it, that's wonderfully insane, right?

One of the most brilliant ways I've seen students "stay foolish" is through work in the Thiel Fellowship (thielfellowship.org) program. Named after billionaire Peter A. Thiel, this fellowship gives young people the time and space to create something new n-o-w. Peter was an early investor in Facebook and co-founder of PayPal, so he knows the value of putting his dollar behind a hot idea and jumping on it like a trampoline. His two-year blueprint offers participants a hundred thousand dollars to study, research, and develop a killer project that'll improve the world via science, tech, and business. The catch? Students under the age of twenty have to leave college to do it. They can go back to finish their degree later, of course, but the point is to work on this strategy now, instead of *after* graduation. This takes guts.

I wonder how Eden Full broke the news to her parents about temporarily dropping out of Princeton University. In 2011, Eden became a Thiel Fellow, one of the first, and invented the SunSaluter, a solar panel tracker that brings forty percent more clean energy and water to villages in nine developing countries. According to her website, the gravity-powered equipment is inexpensive, easy to assemble, and "filters at least four liters of water per day." It was a huge risk for the mechanical engineer from Canada to be part of that very first fellowship class, and it paid off big time. Eden won a bunch of awards, including Ashoka's Youth Social Entrepreneur Award in 2012. Don't be intimidated by Eden's story. We're not all wired to engineer solar panels; that's her path, and you have yours. The point is, staying hungry and foolish may seem difficult, but the outcomes can be incredible if you're willing to take a leap of faith.

★★★ Star Tips ★★★

1. **Sign up:** Find a free or affordable class in person or online. Girls Who Code (girlswhocode.com) is all about closing the gender gap in tech and engineering. They have clubs in middle and high schools and universities around the country, including Florida, New Hampshire, Virginia, Michigan, Arizona, and California. The girls build mobile apps and games. They also have a summer immersion program. Penn State's College of Communications (comm.psu.edu) has a summer communications camp for teens to explore broadcast and multimedia journalism, film, and video.

2. **Read something:** The best part about reading is that you don't have to trek to the library or bookstore for a book. With e-readers, you just download a novel and in minutes, it's yours. The same way you scoop up iTunes gift cards, consider asking for a bookstore or Amazon gift card for your b'day or the holidays to feed your creative jones. Quit thinking that you'll have to decipher themes from *The Great Gatsby*. In school you're handed a required reading list, but what are you pushing yourself to read?

3. **Find a tutorial:** Google and YouTube are your besties. Shoot, they're my besties. There's a YouTube video for practically everything, from baking sinful chocolate chip cookies to dancing tutorials to unlocking your car door when the keys are stuck inside. (I actually searched for that last one when my keys were locked in my jeep during one of NYC's nasty snowstorms.) It's easy to get sucked into watching videos of tiny hamsters eating burritos on YouTube (guilty as charged), but there's also an anime tutorial out there begging to be viewed.

4. **Talk to people:** You have not, because you ask not. Take a break from devouring peanut butter cups (my fave!) and introduce yourself to your auntie's college roommate, the one who's opening up her third fitness club. Don't just admire what she's accomplished from a distance: Ask for an introduction and compliment her entrepreneurial drive. Then tell her about your plan to open a dog grooming business, and pick her brain about how much sweat, money, and time it took to open her very first gym.

5. **Write it down:** So simple, yet so powerful. A list. A plan. A lyric. A goal. Writing it down unclogs your mental plumbing and can be the first step to making something dope happen—like signing up for a bike tour—because it gives you clarity (hey, now I understand!), direction (hey, I'm headed this way!), and focus (hey, that's a distraction!).

Breakin' Bad: Genius At Work

At birth you were given a fresh page to write on, a space to draw your unique story. Little did you know that the world has a bunch of preexisting rules that frown on coloring outside the lines. As time passed, you exerted independence, preferring to eat the mushy pear and banana combo to the carrot and kale mix. Months later, your parents childproofed the house so you weren't introduced to the finer points of gravity by tumbling headfirst down a flight of stairs. The kitchen became forbidden territory because the stove was hot. Still, you explored, because at that age the no-nos in life were very tempting. They still are.

Before you start waving your flag like Tris Prior from *Divergent*, understand that the majority of the rules exist for a reason and are for our protection—or else we'd have complete mayhem in these streets (most likely from people screaming "YOLO"). Sometimes, the guidelines become outdated because no one bothered to revise them as times changed. That can definitely keep anyone from achieving next-level greatness.

My family loves board games and we know the instructions for the ones we play regularly, like Guesstures, Scattegories, and Scrabble, but there are certain rules for each game that are absolutely annoying. So my fam remixes them to create a new set of standards. However, if we're playing with friends we stick to what's on the box. Understanding and mastering the rules is important before whipping out a lil' snap, crackle, and pop. This applies to real-life situations too. This isn't the hall pass to start bullying classmates, spazzing on teachers, or losing your mind. We break bad the smart way, when the technology has blown past our current situation or the rules stifle creativity.

Remember when Beyoncé broke the Internet in 2013 by releasing a self-titled visual album without any marketing? Talk about clever. While the competition thought Jay Z was rubbing sunscreen on Bey's back on a snazzy yacht in Europe, she was gathering producers and musicians for a secret project. Her goal? To rework the industry standard that required months of buildup and the label's approval. This was her fifth album, so Bey knew the blueprint, plus she'd done the usual promo thing before with the Destiny's Child albums. With *Beyoncé*, she posted an Instagram video alerting us that fourteen songs and seventeen videos were available right now. She released that album at midnight on iTunes and the BeyHive (and the rest of the world) went macadamia nuts. Bey used social media to spread the word, not the record label, and the album shot to the top of the charts in several countries.

Twitter went crazy and the celebrity tweets were pretty entertaining:

"Don't talk to me today unless it's about @Beyoncé. Thx." **–Katy Perry**

"I'm literally FUH-REAKING out over this new #Beyoncé... The music vids?!! I can't handle this much fierceness. #NOJOKE #DYING." **–Demi Lovato**

"What can't Beyoncé do? #queen #newalbum #merryxmastome."
–Eva Amurri Martino

The music and videos were pure fire. She had us chanting we "woke up like dis," and claiming that we were "flawless." But more importantly, Bey, doing what few singers could've done, lit a stick of dynamite under the rules—and changed the game.

If I'm talking about game changers, then I gotta throw Netflix into the mix. Before this service popped up, people trekked to their local Blockbuster to rent and return movies, deal with rude employees, and pay late fees. Netflix flipped it. Their videos arrived at your house in a red envelope with a prepaid sleeve to return the new Jennifer Lopez flick. And guess what? No late fees. In business, the way to succeed is to be the fastest, the cheapest, or the best in your field. That means study the competition. Netflix examined everything Blockbuster did wrong. Meanwhile, Blockbuster slept on Netflix and just plain failed to see them as a threat. That's not to say that Netflix is perfect, but the idea of jumping onto emerging technologies now rather than later was important to becoming a million dollar baby.

And they constantly evolve. In 2007, they started streaming movies and by 2011 Netflix started acquiring original content. They gave us a chance to watch the entire season of a new show, like *House of Cards* or *Orange Is the New Black*, in one sitting—while the old model had us waiting for the following week. Mind you, I'd been gobbling up back-to-back *Law & Order* reruns on TNT and *Honeymooners* marathons every New Year's Eve for years. But when Netflix made this an option with something new, it became known as binge watching. Groundbreaking? Abso-freakin'-lutely. No matter who tests the limits of an idea or breaks the rules, the mastermind deals with the consequences and stands behind her (or his) decision when the results are amazing or disastrous. My advice: Use your power for good.

Sometimes people break the rules on your behalf, because talent shouldn't be limited because of a "this is how it's always been done" mentality. This automatically makes me think of Jennifer Lee. She co-directed the box-office hit *Frozen*. Little girls ran around in Elsa and Anna costumes warbling "Let It Go" off-key. They probably had no idea that Jennifer was the first woman in Walt Disney Animations studio history to direct an animated film—and the first writer at any major animation studio to rock the director's cap. The normal path in her business is to start as an animator or story artist and climb the ranks to a feature film. But Jennifer was tapped to write *Frozen* while finishing up *Wreck-It-Ralph*. Today, Jennifer is the proud owner of an Oscar for *Frozen* (Best Animated Feature Film) and has the honor of being the first female director to have a film zoom pass the one billion dollar box office earnings mark.

What do Eden Full, Beyoncé, Netflix, and Jennifer Lee have in common? Imagination and vision. Both are powerful. Mark Zuckerberg and his college buddies whipped up Facebook (originally called Facemash) while at Harvard University. Look around. What can problem can you fix? How can you bring people together? Facebook initially started as a way for Harvard kids to connect. Then it expanded to other Boston colleges and later, other Ivy

League schools. Now, more than nine hundred million people use it, including your grandfather. Start breaking some rules (the good kind!) with your big idea.

And The Rule Breaker Award Goes To...

List Your Top Three Rule Breakers

1. _____

2. _____

3. _____

How did she (or he) change the game (i.e. their industry, culture, social media, or life in general)?

1. _____

_____

_____

_____

_____

_____

2. _____

_____

_____

3. _____

What did you learn from their creative genius—or their mistakes?

1. _____

2. _____

_____

_____

_____

_____

_____

_____

3. _____

_____

_____

_____

_____

_____

Where will you use your imagination to change the game? How will you accomplish this?

_____

_____

_____

_____

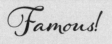

Famous!

CHEAT SHEET NO. 10

My plan to get up, get out and get more is:

_____

_____

_____

_____

_____

One step toward achieving this goal is:

_____

_____

_____

_____

I promise that I'll:

_____

_____

_____

_____

_____

Before You Go

As you wrap up *Famous!*, know that your journey begins now. I hope you're inspired, ready to put some of my tips into practice, and eager to #bethestarofyourshow.

You've devoured lots of new info, and may feel a little overwhelmed by what you've read, or amped to get started on mapping out your next accomplishment. Both reactions are okay and normal. I have some suggestions on moving forward, and it doesn't matter if you ate Courage Corn Flakes or Lost in the Sauce Fruit Loops for breakfast.

First, **take some time to be quiet and unplug.** Thirty minutes should be good. This means no texts, selfies, or tweets. Silence scares most of us because we're suddenly forced to pay attention to the many thoughts fighting for attention in our head. During one of my silent moments, I realized that I'm an ambivert. That's an SAT word for a person with both introvert and extrovert traits. I enjoy introducing myself to strangers at parties, the same way I love to sit in my living room and read a book for hours. For your quiet time, allow what you've read to sink in. That Bragging List may have been challenging because it isn't part of your DNA to celebrate your accomplishments. Remember that it is healthy and positive to recognize your gifts. Shoot, there's a victory parade when athletes win a big game. Take a minute to think about three, just three, awesome things you've done, and add them to the list when your thirty minutes are up. Include the time you saved a toddler from drowning or when your group won the Best in State Verizon Innovative App Challenge. You know what to write. Do it.

Second, **do something today your future self will thank you for.** This can be anything. Maybe you finally block that irritating troll on IG who made cracks about your weight. Maybe you decide to start a step team at your school because the cheerleaders are so wack and you were diagnosed as wacktose intolerant. Maybe you go back and fill out that Fave Five activity. Yeah, you thought I didn't see you zoom past that to the next chapter, right? I did. Focus on who should be on that list. Who are the best candidates for those slots? Can The Seer really envision your career as an architect? Will The Treasurer loan you a hundred bucks to start your T-shirt business. Your future self will be grateful that you didn't allow trolls to mess with your self-esteem, took the initiative to start something new, and decided who were the best people to consult for advice.

Third, **remember my five core beliefs**. This is what I live by, so feel free to adopt, remix, or write your own. You know I don't believe in perfection; mistakes are proof that you're trying. So here are those beliefs once more, in case you forgot:

Confidence is your best accessory. Retail therapy is a temporary fix to any problem. The real power boost needed to slay the day comes from *believing* you can do it, *acting* like you can do, and then *doing* it. This doesn't just happen once, either. You have to believe, act and do on a daily basis.

Advice from your Fave Five is essential. You've selected these people to be your personal advisory board, so put them to use regularly. Talk to them about your challenges, dreams, and goals. The Social Butterfly may have an opportunity for a bright high school student (okay, that's you!) to intern in the mayor's office this summer, but you've fallen completely off her radar. Why? Because the last time she heard from you was New Year's Eve. Stay in touch and come bearing gifts. Does she run on Dunkin? Send The Social Butterfly a ten-dollar gift card to her favorite coffee bar and she'll think of you while sipping her java.

Choose your own adventure. Stay in the city to attend college or travel five hundred miles away? Create the best promposal ever or let that cutie you've adored for years dance with someone else at the last high school hurrah? Decisions, decisions. Think about it. Weigh the pros and cons. Create scenarios. Trust your gut. Eat courage for breakfast and go do something awesome, like attend New York University because you're a country girl by birth but a city girl at heart. Or accept that academic scholarship to Spelman College in Atlanta because it means you're just a three-hour drive from home. Life isn't one size fits all. It's a custom fit and what works for your bestie may not suit your needs. Choose what feels right for *you*... and think about Bethany Hamilton. When she was 13 years old she went surfing (she'd learned the sport a few years prior) and a fifteen-foot tiger shark bit off her arm. That could've been a wrap for Bethany, because surfers need two arms, right? What if she allowed fear of failure to keep her on the sand—instead of in the ocean? What if she allowed doubt to creep in? What if she believed that surfing wasn't part of her future anymore? Well, one month after the shark attack, Bethany was back in the water and on her board. Two years later, she won first place in the Explorer Women's Division of the NSSA Championships. Bethany chose her own adventure and she knew it included surfing.

Failure is a part of success. This is a hard truth to swallow, but possibly the most important. The sooner you get used to it, the sooner you'll appreciate life's lessons. Everything won't always go your way. You won't always win the championship game. You won't pass the Big Test. But these letdowns shouldn't break you. Promise me that you'll strive to get stronger each time.

Define yourself for yourself. You're the author of your life story. The best part is the definition is constantly changing and evolving. Hey, look at me, I thought I'd bring home Olympic gold in double Dutch. Yeah, not so much. But I'm fine with that. Being a writer, editor, and speaker suits me much better. Reject boxes and labels (band girl, geek, weirdo, jock) because you're complex and have multiple layers like those yummy cakes your grandfather bakes for your birthday. Don't allow anyone to tell you who you are. You're choosing your own adventure, failing, succeeding, checking in with the Fave Five, rocking a confidence glow, and adding more text to your pages. Attempt to pen a new six-word memoir every day. Today's entry: I'm awesome. Let me show you.

Rock With Me On Social Media

Okay, so I hope you realize that our relationship doesn't stop here. Oh, no, we're stuck together now. In the beginning of the book, I told you that I've been you're A-1 since Day-1 and I meant it. Let's connect on social media. Follow me (@TaiiaSmartYoung) on Instagram, Twitter, and Snapchat and use #bethestarofyourshow. If there's a private matter you need to get off your chest, hit me up on my website (TaiiaSmartYoung.com), so we can work it out or simply sign up on my site for tips and freebies. If you want to see my mug live and in person, 'cause let's face it I'm kinda cute, invite me to your city for a Be the Star of Your Show Workshop, to speak at your youth conference, or attend the invite-only book signing for *Famous!* that you whipped up with one of your Fave Five. Fill out the form on the contact page of my site and let's make it happen.

Thank you for allowing me to be a part of your journey. I can't wait to hear about your adventures. March bravely into the world, accomplish something amazing, and don't ever forget to #bethestarofyourshow.